SISTERS, *arise!*

SISTERS, arise!

Becoming the Woman God Intends You to Be

LYNNE PERRY CHRISTOFFERSON

Covenant Communications, Inc.

Covenant®

Cover image: *Spring Flowers* © Daniel Rodríguez Quintana, courtesy istockphoto.com

Cover design copyright © 2016 by Covenant Communications, Inc.

Published by Covenant Communications, Inc.
American Fork, Utah

Printed in the United States of America
First Printing: March 2016

21 20 19 18 17 16   10 9 8 7 6 5 4 3 2 1

ISBN 978-1-68047-937-9

Joni

Happy Mothers Day!

You are such a caring mother and work so hard to teach and train your two girls. It's the most important job you will ever have. As you already know it is exhausting work but has rewarding joy as you watch your children grow. We love you!

Lynn & Debbie

P.S. This woman came and spoke at our womens conference for the Stake last year. She was so humble and sincere, I bought her book. I think you will like it too ♡

2018

This book is dedicated to
Janice Kapp Perry,
my remarkably unworldly mother,
and
Sarah, Rebecca, and Kate,
my daughters who were first my sisters

ACKNOWLEDGMENTS

My sincere thanks go to a handful of women put in my path at critical moments of the writing journey: Heather Griffin, Roxanne Thayne, Emily Freeman, Kristen Smeltzer, and Janice Kapp Perry. I consider your beautiful lives to be blueprints for the woman I am trying to become.

Deep appreciation goes to my husband, Bradley Christofferson, who kindly prevented his low-tech wife from taking a baseball bat to the computer on more than one occasion and whose timely bit of writing counsel made all the difference. To my five children I give gratitude for patience with me and for the occasional vigorous back scratch during the slow process of bringing my ideas to fruition.

I thank the Covenant Communications team for magically transforming my humble manuscript into an actual book. To my editor, Stacey Turner, I give particular thanks for pleasantly answering my endless stream of questions and for the light touch with which she polished my sentences.

Lastly, thank you to the human who invented the Undo feature of my word-processing program. You have no idea how many times you saved my bacon!

Section One
EMBRACING OUR ORIGINS

CHAPTER #1
Sisters, Arise!

BLAME IT ON THE WIMPLES and crisping pins—they got me riding this train of thought. There I was, an unsuspecting seminary student, just minding my own business, when suddenly I came face-to-face with chapter 13 of 2 Nephi. You know, one of the dreaded *Isaiah chapters*. Though most of the verses were going right over my head, my ears perked up when the instructor read about "the daughters of Zion" (2 Nephi 13:16). Did that refer to me? I thought it might, so I began listening in earnest: "Because the daughters of Zion are haughty, and walk with stretched-forth necks and wanton eyes . . ." Whoa! I was pretty sure that wasn't a compliment.

I continued reading on my own, discovering a most unusual list. Among other things, Isaiah referred to "tinkling ornaments, and cauls, and round tires like the moon . . . the mantles, and the wimples, and the crisping-pins" (2 Nephi 13:18, 22). Did he say "wimples"? According to my seminary teacher, everything Isaiah listed was either an item of clothing or a type of accessory or adornment used by females. Apparently, the females he was referring to were inclined to seriously overaccessorize. But that was only an outward symbol of a much deeper issue. Reading the chapter again in my bedroom that night, I concluded that there would come a time when at least some of the women of Christ's church would become extremely worldly and materialistic. Verse 4 of the next chapter referred to "the filth of the daughters of Zion" (2 Nephi 14:4). This idea was very troubling to my young heart. Would there really come a day when the covenant daughters of Zion actually became filthy?

In the years since my experience in seminary, I have studied the words of Isaiah enough to know that much of what he wrote has many layers of meaning. While I'm no expert on his writings, I feel certain that one of the layers in this particular chapter was a forecast of an approaching storm of worldliness—a forecast Latter-day Saint women would be wise to study. If I am not mistaken, the storm is already here.

Fast forward two decades from seminary. One Sunday, my stake president showed up in our Relief Society unannounced. He asked if he could take five minutes to speak at the end of the meeting. What he had to say was so unexpected and made such a deep impression on me that I remember it vividly years later: "Sisters, my counselors and I issue temple recommends to the women of our stake, and then we see you downtown at the store or the ballgame. We're troubled that so many of you are dressed in clothing that you could not possibly wear unless you've removed your temple garments or altered them in some way." He paused and then said words that burned into my mind: "The worldliness of our sisters is *poisoning* our daughters."

Ouch! No beating around the bush here. Yet his words were not spoken in an accusing tone. These were the words of an inspired priesthood leader who was so concerned for the sisters under his stewardship that he dared to come say the hard thing.

Thinking back on Isaiah's prophecy, I suspect mine is not the only stake of the Church where worldly attitudes may be creeping in.

Sisters, arise! At some point, as covenant women in the last days, we must admit to ourselves that it is not enough to be *less immodest* than pop culture dictates. Being less immodest is not the same thing as actually being modest. In the Lord's eyes, being *less worldly* in our dress, speech, and behavior is not the same as being *unworldly*. We may deceive ourselves into believing we should be congratulated for walking several steps behind the rest of the population in terms of worldliness, but the fact remains that if we're on the same path as the world, we will eventually reach the same destructive end. It really doesn't matter who gets there first.

As Sister Margaret Nadauld clearly stated: "Women of God can never be like women of the world. The world has enough women who are tough; we need women who are tender. There are enough women who are coarse; we need women who are kind. There are enough women who are rude; we need women who are refined. We have enough women of fame and fortune; we need more women of faith. We have enough greed; we need more goodness. We have enough vanity; we need more virtue. We have enough popularity; we need more purity."[1] You may have heard those words before. I think they cannot be quoted enough.

But what's the big deal with following the rest of the world? Aside from jeopardizing our eternal welfare and our ability to have access to the influence of the Holy Spirit? Aside from *that*? Reflect for a moment on your personal struggles and challenges, the pain and heartbreak you have faced in your lifetime, and your constant battles to overcome the "natural woman" as you're tempted on every side. Life can be *so* tough. But if you think *you* have it hard, just imagine the struggles and despair of those who are enduring their trials without the benefit of a living prophet, the gift of the Holy Ghost, the Book of Mormon, the priesthood, and the holy temple. I tremble to even contemplate a life without these blessings.

This is why it is critical that the women of the restored Church reflect Jesus Christ in our actions and in our countenances—so others will recognize in us something different from what the world is offering and turn to us for hope and help in navigating their modern minefields. So many earnest seekers are kept from the truth only because "they know not where to find it" (D&C 123:12).

We claim to be witnesses for the Savior, so why are so many of us trying so hard to look and act in ways that don't accurately represent Him? My purpose in writing is not to pass judgment but to encourage an increased focus on turning from harmful, worldly fads and beginning a better trend—one that reflects our devotion to Jesus Christ.

I share the conviction of Sister Sheri Dew: "We are here to influence the world rather than to be influenced by the world. If we could unleash the full influence of covenant-keeping women, the kingdom of God would change overnight."[2]

Sisters, arise! Could a stranger discern, just by observing our appearance and actions, that we are women of covenant? If not, why not? Perhaps we have fallen victim to a serious case of spiritual identity fraud. Maybe we are buying into Satan's whisperings that we are weak or inferior to men—that our value is determined by our degree of physical attractiveness. How damaging to our spirits to view ourselves in this way, and how offensive to our Heavenly Father, who expects so much more from his daughters.

I have a treasured image in my mind, a mental video clip stored from my college days: Dance students surround me in a large gym. The graceful young teacher stands before us and demonstrates a simple move that leaves me nearly breathless—it is *that* beautiful. Slowly, she rises on the toes of one foot while extending her other leg slightly behind. Her arms flow gradually outward, wing-like. Her chest rises with a smooth intake of breath, while her neck pulls slightly back. It's as if something inside her is expanding, and her body is stretching to accommodate the change. For just a moment, she appears to be contemplating flight. This is what I picture when I say, "Sisters, arise!"—a physical representation of an inward movement.

Imagine our spirits rising up in this same way as we recognize the power and beauty of purity, and our ability to effect change in the world around us. *Everyone* benefits from the strength and influence of a godly woman.

I say *enough* with the wimples and crisping pins and all they represent! Enough with whatever is preventing us from caring more about the condition of our spirits than the state of our wardrobes. Enough of pursuing the expendable at the expense of the essential. It's time to put down the fashion magazine and pick up the *Ensign*, to search the scriptures as eagerly as we do a best-selling novel, to exit the chat room and enter the temple. It's high time we live up to both our privileges and our responsibilities. Sisters, arise!

Notes

1 Margaret D. Nadauld, "The Joy of Womanhood," *Ensign*, November 2000.

2 Sheri L. Dew, BYU Women's Conference, May 1, 2008, http://ce.byu.edu/cw/ womensconference/transcripts.php.

CHAPTER #2
Our Soul's Awakening

IF WORLDLINESS IS POISON, WHAT is its antidote? I believe it is this: We must understand exactly who we are. Women who catch the vision of their divine roots are never completely content to live beneath their potential. We may do our best to ignore the inner voice that whispers that we are better than that, and the natural tendencies of our mortal bodies may frequently wrestle with our bright spirits, but "The Spirit itself beareth witness with our spirit, that we are the children of God" (Romans 8:16).

I have a favorite story, wherein a moment of revelation changed the course of a life, and that life has now inspired millions of people:

She was born in Alabama, just as bright and healthy as any other child and, by all accounts, rather precocious. She learned to roll over, to crawl, and then to take her first teetering steps—her new mobility enabling her to begin exploring the small world of her home and yard. Her tiny lips were just beginning to form a few short words: da-da, wah-wah (water). Then a thief, in the form of a raging fever, nearly took her life. As the fever finally abated and it became clear that the child would live, the devastating discovery was made that little Helen Keller had been robbed of both hearing and sight.

Who can imagine the confusion and panic she experienced, waking up to a black and silent world? No longer could she see the familiar faces of her parents, hear their words of comfort, or communicate her feelings and needs in the usual ways. Week by week, year after year, her frustration mounted until she became wild—nearly unmanageable—in her attempts to break free from the constraints of her condition.

At age seven she received a great blessing in the form of a remarkably patient and determined young teacher, Anne Sullivan. Helen would later write that she considered the day Anne came into her life as her real birthday. The first month together was exhausting for both teacher and student as Anne showed Helen, in no uncertain terms, that kicking and screaming would not be tolerated as methods of communication. Gradually, as Helen grew more docile, Anne began teaching her the manual alphabet by spelling into Helen's hand. Bright as the young girl was, she still struggled to grasp the concept that the letters formed words and the words represented specific objects.

On April 5, 1887, Helen made a discovery that changed the course of her life. Her teacher took her to the pump house and had Helen hold a jug under the spout. Anne pumped while spelling w-a-t-e-r into Helen's free hand. According to Anne, "The word coming so close upon the sensation of cold water rushing over [Helen's] hand seemed to startle her. She dropped the jug and stood as one transfixed. A new light came into her face."[1]

Helen had made a connection. She recalled that as a toddler she had known a word for that liquid: *wah-wah*—WATER! She later wrote, "Suddenly I felt a misty consciousness as of something forgotten—a thrill of returning thought; and somehow the mystery of language was revealed to me. I knew then that w-a-t-e-r meant that wonderful cool something that was flowing over my hand. That living word awakened my soul, gave it light, hope, joy, set it free! There were barriers still, it is true, but barriers that could in time be swept away."[2] Her new understanding of the workings of language gave Helen hope of communicating freely with others and the possibility of rising above her current limitations. By evening of the same day she had learned thirty new words.

We could discuss—for hours—Helen Keller's marvelous accomplishments: her academic achievements, world travels, eloquent writing, circle of famous friends, and impressive inroads she made as an advocate for the rights of women and for the disabled. But for me, Helen's story is all about a single moment of revelation, a fleeting glimpse which forever altered her future. She refers to this singular experience as "my soul's . . . awakening."[3]

I submit that as women of this last dispensation, we have a deep need for our own spiritual awakening—a powerful realization that "we are the offspring of God" (Acts 17:29). Helen's revelation was triggered by water literally flowing over her hand, stirring a memory. Perhaps our awakening will come as living water rushes over our minds and seeps into our spirits, like "a misty consciousness as of something forgotten"—a vague remembrance of who we were before our time on earth. It will likely not be an astonishing, one-time occurrence. Rather, it will be the cumulative effect of studying and listening to the truth about who we really are—truth gleaned from Sunday School and seminary and scriptures, from family nights and firesides, from hymn singing and heartfelt praying. As we're exposed repeatedly to light and truth, they will eventually penetrate our very core.

Alluding to our divine origins, Elder Glenn L. Pace quotes the beautiful hymn text of Eliza R. Snow:

> When I leave this frail existence,
> When I lay this mortal by,
> Father, Mother, may I meet you
> In your royal courts on high?[4]

Elder Pace continues, "Sisters, I testify that when you stand in front of your heavenly parents in those royal courts on high and look into *Her* eyes and behold *Her* countenance, any question you ever had about the role of women in the kingdom will evaporate into the rich celestial air because at that moment you will see standing directly in front of you your divine nature and destiny."[5]

Helen Keller wrote, "During the first nineteen months of my life I had caught glimpses of broad, green fields, a luminous sky, trees and flowers which the darkness that followed could not wholly blot out."[6] The fact that Helen had once been able to see enabled her to have what I would call "inner vision" even after she became physically blind. Referring to Anne Sullivan's pivotal role in opening up her student's world, Helen stated:

"The most important day I remember in all my life is the one on which my teacher . . . came to me. I am filled with wonder when I consider the immeasurable contrast between the two lives which it connects."[7]

In a similar fashion, the life of purpose we can live once we've gained a true sense of our premortal roots and divine potential stands in stark contrast to the life we lived prior to receiving this sacred knowledge.

Somewhere, locked within our spirits, are memories of our pre-earth life and an understanding of our true nature. Sisters, we must make a connection as Helen did. Though we will likely not have any visual memories of our pre-earth life, the Spirit will whisper to us that our nature is divine, that we existed long before our mortal birth, and that we have a work to do in building God's kingdom.

As God's daughters who lived in His presence before coming to earth, it is certain that there was a time when we had no questions about our identity. Our spiritual blindness is partly "Fall induced" and partly the result of the veil. What, then, could be more important than participating in activities that thin the veil? Gradually, we can experience, as Helen Keller did, "a misty consciousness as of something forgotten—a thrill of returning thought."

Speaking of the need for the women of the Church to live up to their promises, Elder M. Russell Ballard has written the following thought-provoking lines:

> When God asked who would come to earth to prepare a way for all mankind to be saved and strengthened and blessed, it was Jesus Christ who said, simply, "Here am I, send me" (Abraham 3:27). Just as the Savior stepped forward to fulfill His divine responsibilities, we have the challenge and responsibility to do likewise. If you are wondering if you make a difference to the Lord, imagine the impact when you make commitments such as the following:
>
> "Father, if you need a woman to rear children in righteousness, here am I, send me.
>
> "If you need a woman who will shun vulgarity and dress modestly and speak with dignity and show the world how joyous it is to keep the commandments, here am I, send me.
>
> "If you need a woman who can resist the alluring temptations of the world by keeping her eyes fixed on eternity, here am I, send me. . . ."

Between now and the day the Lord comes again, He needs women in every family, in every ward, in every community, in every nation, who will step forward in righteousness and say by their words and their actions, "Here am I, send me."[8]

Imagine the power and impact of an entire generation of sisters supporting each other in purity, demonstrating that the influence of virtuous women can send ripples of righteousness flowing to every corner of the earth. As our souls are awakened to the breathtaking truth of our eternal identity, we will desire to rise up and be women of holiness, consistent with our divine roots.

Notes

1 Helen Keller, *The Story of My Life* (New York, London: W.W. Norton, 2003), 150.
2 Ibid., 27–28.
3 Ibid., 28.
4 "O, My Father," *Hymns of The Church of Jesus Christ of Latter-day Saints* (Salt Lake City: The Church of Jesus Christ of Latter-day Saints, 1985) no. 292.
5 Glenn L. Pace, The Divine Nature and Destiny of Women," BYU Devotional, March 6, 2010, http://speeches.byu.edu, emphasis added.
6 Helen Keller, *The Story of My Life* (New York, London: W.W. Norton, 2003), 27.
7 Ibid., 25.
8 M. Russell Ballard, "Here Am I, Send Me," http://speeches.byu.edu.

CHAPTER #3
They Don't Take Visa

They don't take Visa at the temple. I know this for a fact. It was mid-December, and I was knee-deep in holiday preparations. I'd whipped out my trusty Visa debit card countless times during a week of serious Christmas shopping, so it was only natural that I would pull it out at the recommend desk of the temple, right?

When the white-haired gentleman at the counter just smiled and gently shook his head, I glanced down to see if my recommend had expired, and realized my mistake. Sheepishly, I tucked the card back in my wallet and produced my temple recommend. They *do* take those.

This incident had a tremendous impact on me. I was ashamed to admit how casual I had become with my temple attendance. Hoping to squeeze my regular endowment session into a jam-packed holiday schedule, I had charged into the lobby of the temple without a single thought for the sacredness of the experience that was available there. Years later, when I heard the following words from Elder David A. Bednar, I knew exactly what he meant: "There is a difference between church-attending, tithe-paying members who occasionally rush into the temple to go through a session and those members who faithfully and consistently worship in the temple."[1]

Though my Visa incident was a motivating factor in changing my approach to attending the temple, it was not the only one. Several months after that experience, I was wondering how to access wisdom and even heavenly intervention on behalf of one of my children. I learned that my brother, Robb, had volunteered to be an ordinance worker at the temple. Knowing how busy he was with his job and growing young family, I felt some surprise that he would be willing to donate six or seven hours of his time each week. It occurred to me that if a busy man like Robb was making this sacrifice, surely *I* could make the time to attend the temple more frequently. The Spirit whispered that this was a way to obtain blessings for my struggling child.

Around this time, as I sat in sacrament meeting, I heard a speaker quote a letter written several years before by the First Presidency: "Where time and circumstances permit, members are encouraged to *replace some leisure activities with temple service.*"[2] Instantly, I thought of my circumstances: My children were all in school five days a week. I was not employed. I actually had free time on my hands. My health was good, and I lived in close proximity to several temples. What excuse did I have for not being in the temple frequently? There was none. I left the chapel that day determined to increase my temple attendance significantly.

Sounds easy on paper, doesn't it? Well, it wasn't. I went to the temple that Friday and penciled future visits on my calendar so I wouldn't forget. As I prepared for bed the night before my next scheduled trip, I realized that the next morning was my day to be in the temple again. *Already?* I confess that for the first few months I was rather hit-and-miss in my efforts. There was always a reason to postpone my next visit to the temple: I was too tired, I had the sniffles, the weather was nasty, my children were out of school, it was too close to Christmas, I forgot to launder my temple dress, the temple was closed for cleaning (never mind that there were other temples within an easy drive). I used excuse after lame excuse. But after several months of increased attendance, I noticed something—I was finding it harder and harder to justify my attempts to stay home.

A year after beginning this process, I realized that when I missed my scheduled temple day, I felt anxious to return. After several years, I admitted to myself that other than sickness or emergency, I had no excuse good enough to justify staying home. When I finally made that determination, temple attendance became a pleasure. I began doing initiatory work alternately with endowments and found myself moved by the beautiful words of that ordinance. In recent years I've added baptisms and sealing ordinances as well. Call me a late bloomer, but finally—in middle age—I can say that I truly rejoice in temple service.

Although it has taken years to develop this feeling, I actually began to see blessings flow into my life almost immediately after making the initial effort to increase my temple attendance. I have received insights on behalf of my family and deep spiritual comfort when I've desperately needed it. But the blessing I notice most often is that I have become "aware." Every hour spent in the temple seems to translate into a growing awareness of my standing before the Lord, both in terms of progress I have made and in the ways I need to change.

Nowhere is our true identity more apparent than in the house of the Lord. In no other place do we feel so connected to those around us. The more time we spend in the peaceful, uncluttered atmosphere of the temple, where modesty and simplicity prevail, the more we become aware of the contrast between the Lord's ways and the ways of the world. We strengthen our ability to keep our covenants each time we renew them.

As I've reflected on the tremendous blessings that have come to me from improved temple worship, it hardly seems fair that so many Church members must travel significant distances to reach the nearest temple. For some it is actually a once-in-a-lifetime experience. After stewing over this for some time, I've come to two conclusions. The first: I have absolutely no excuse not to serve in the temple on a regular basis. The second: I think the "manna principle" applies here.

After Moses led the children of Israel out of Egypt, the people complained that they didn't have enough food. The Lord told them He would "rain bread from heaven" for them to eat. Everyone was to gather just enough to use each day—anything left over would get worms in it and stink. Seriously! But something surprising occurred every week. On the sixth day Moses's people were to gather twice as much manna, and what was left over did not spoil as on other days but provided food for the Sabbath. (See Exodus 16:2–25.)

What could that possibly have to do with the temple? Well, those who have easy access to a temple are able to gather spiritual manna there on a regular basis. For those who are farther away, but make the effort to attend whenever possible, the Lord can make that nourishment last longer. I don't believe this principle applies to those of us who go to the temple but give it little thought afterward. But it does apply to those who frequently review their temple covenants in their minds and seek to keep them, who search out what the scriptures teach on the subject, and who study the words of the living prophets with regard to temple worship. The manna *they* receive at the temple can last as long as it's needed.

One unexpected lesson I learned through increased temple attendance is that simply being in the temple more often does not automatically give us a better grasp of the endowment. Yes, we do receive blessings each time we attend and we are doing an important work for our brothers and sisters beyond the veil, but unless we are more than a warm body in a chair, our understanding will remain at a basic level. I know this firsthand since I still struggle in this area.

The Lord does not reveal the doctrines of the temple lightly, but when He perceives that we are seeking truth, focused on the ordinances, and striving diligently to keep our covenants, He will share "line upon line; here a little, and there a little" (Isaiah 28:10).

I cannot emphasize enough that *everyone's journey to improved temple worship will be as different as our circumstances.* Age, health, employment, finances, family situations, and distance all have an effect on our ability to attend the temple. Sometimes it isn't the frequency of our visits that needs to change but the *quality* of our experience.

Want to hear the rest of my Visa story? A few years after that embarrassing incident, I stood in the checkout line of my grocery store, ready to pay for a cart full of food. Without conscious thought, I fished the leather wallet out of my purse and was halfway to handing the clerk my temple recommend when I realized my mistake. This time, however, I felt no embarrassment as I slipped the recommend back in its place and produced my Visa card. They *do* take those.

The clerk must have wondered about the silly grin on my face, but I offered no explanation. I was basking in the evidence that my approach to worshipping in the temple had changed. No longer was the temple simply a place I visited—it was becoming a way of life. It had taken several years and much conscious effort, but I had progressed from a woman who stood at the temple recommend desk preoccupied by Christmas shopping, to one who stood in line at the grocery store thinking about the temple. (Okay, so sometimes I notice the candy bars too, but still . . .)

Notes

1 David A. Bednar, "Honorably Hold a Name and Standing," *Ensign*, May 2009.
2 Letter from The First Presidency, The Church of Jesus Christ of Latter-day Saints, March 11, 2003, emphasis added.

Section Two
HONORING OUR BODIES

CHAPTER #4
When the Lord Makes You Over

PICTURE THIS: A MOUSY-HAIRED, TWENTY-SOMETHING female window-shops downtown on her lunch hour. Suddenly, she's ambushed by a TV film crew and literally pulled off the street. For the next four hours, she's put into the hands of style experts. The "victim" receives a trendy haircut and color job; then a makeup artist works a miracle on her face. Finally, a fashion consultant finishes the look with a flattering new outfit and accessories. With the makeover complete, the television cameras capture the stunned reactions of family and friends as the new look is revealed. Years ago, I was intrigued by this program. It was fascinating to witness the transformation from frumpy to fantastic.

There's another makeover trend. It involves making over a person using far more drastic methods. Going way beyond hair and makeup, this program uses plastic surgeries, orthodontic procedures, and fitness training over a period of weeks or months, with results so dramatic that the subjects are almost unrecognizable when compared to their "before" pictures. This trend is disturbing to me, yet I understand the urge to indulge.

Our modern culture has an obsession with makeovers. You name it, someone has probably made it over—their wardrobe, their house, their yard, their high-calorie dessert recipe, even their husband. But good judgment is necessary for any improvement project. Sure, you can replace carpets and slap a coat of paint on the walls, but really, who cares whether your walls are plum or taupe when the plumbing is backed up? In the same way, a little makeup and some carefully chosen clothes can do wonders for our looks, but if we're selfish, undisciplined, or prone to gossip, who's going to care that we look great? The world cares, but is that who we really want to please? And if the answer to that last question is yes, should we be worried?

When it comes to physical makeovers, there's certainly nothing wrong with improving our appearance, but we would do well to pinpoint exactly what we're trying to accomplish. If we make over our bodies in an attempt to find lasting happiness or spiritual satisfaction, good luck. We would be better served by focusing on our "inward parts."

I recall standing at a makeup counter in a department store, searching for a particular shade of lipstick. As I held up a tube to check the name of the color, I had to squint. Still, I couldn't quite make out the words. I tried holding the tube farther away but was still unable to decipher the tiny print. It took a minute to realize I must be in need of reading glasses. This felt like a slap in the face to me because surely it meant I was officially middle-aged. In the ensuing years there have been other, more visible, signs of aging, and I've occasionally found myself tempted to drink from the world's plastic fountain of youth.

Confession: not long after I first noticed evidence of aging on my face, I developed a strange ritual, repeated nightly for several weeks. No, it wasn't a new beauty regimen—there was nothing beautiful about it. Once I slipped on pajamas, brushed teeth, and said my prayers, I would lie in bed obsessing over the fact that the crow's feet around my eyes were sure to be joined any day by sagging jowls, thinning lips, triple chins, and a host of age spots and unsightly growths. I was certain I had read somewhere that cartilage continues to grow until you die—meaning my nose and ears would eventually stretch all out of proportion to the rest of my face. Horrors! The picture these thoughts conjured in my mind was enough to make me panic.

I'm not proud of this fact, but I often drifted off to sleep while making a mental head-to-toe list of what I would change about my body. In my dreams, I underwent several liposuction procedures. You wouldn't believe what a difference they made—until I woke up. After a few weeks of this twisted thinking, I found myself restless and discontent. *So what* that I had a wonderful husband, five bright children, a nice home, great neighbors, the fullness of the gospel, and frequent access to chocolate? What did any of those blessings matter if I was eventually going to wrinkle like a prune?

Even as I write this, I feel sick inside remembering that thought process. Will I continue to age? Yep. The past several years have proven that aging is inevitable. But in large measure my thinking has changed.

Change began as I watched the broadcast of general conference in October 2005. Two talks stood out to me like neon lights because they directly addressed the issues I was wrestling with each night. Sister Susan W. Tanner spoke powerfully about the sanctity of the body, testifying "that the body is a gift to be treated with gratitude and respect."[1] In Elder Jeffrey R. Holland's address, "To Young Women," he said, "In terms of preoccupation with self and a fixation on the physical . . . *it is spiritually destructive.* . . . And if adults are preoccupied with appearance—tucking and nipping and implanting and remodeling everything that can be remodeled—those pressures and anxieties will certainly seep through to children."[2]

These talks made a deep impression as the Spirit bore witness that I was hearing truth. My dissatisfaction had come when I began to entertain the lie that pursuing youth and beauty was worth any cost. That conference weekend I put an end to my destructive nighttime ritual and felt immediate relief in doing so. I bear witness that "the truth shall make you free" (John 8:32).

During the following weeks, I had conversations with several friends which made it clear that I wasn't the only one powerfully impacted by the truths shared by Elder Holland and Sister Tanner. It also became apparent that nearly all of my closest friends, women I consider beautiful by any standard, were struggling in one way or another with their body image and worries about aging.

Sisters, where does this rejection of our bodies and this fear of aging originate? Elder Holland offers this idea: "Frankly, the world has been brutal with you in this regard. You are bombarded in movies, television, fashion magazines, and advertisements with the message that looks are everything!"[3]

The world would have us believe that *plastic makes perfect*—either by waving our magical plastic credit card to buy all the latest beauty potions, spa treatments, and enough wimples and crisping pins to accessorize an elephant, or by going under the knife, because for every flaw we see in the mirror, there is a type of plastic surgery available to "fix it." The lie is that if we can erase our physical imperfections, we'll finally be happy. Sisters, be careful. Satan has our number, and *it is vanity and insecurity*. He knows that, in general, women are remarkably easy to distract with promises of perpetual youth, beauty, and weight loss.

Aside from the physical risk inherent in any surgical procedure, there is even greater spiritual risk when one is making over her body in extreme ways. The urge to display the "new and improved" body by wearing revealing clothing is a powerful temptation for many people. This is not behavior befitting covenant women.

Now, really, who am *I* to tell you to pause before you embark on that slippery slope of plastic surgery? I recognize there are perfectly legitimate reasons for some surgical procedures, and I do not presume to stand as your judge. But since Elder Holland—a prophet, seer, and revelator—has cautioned us on this subject, we would be wise not to indulge in cosmetic surgeries without careful, even prayerful, consideration.

The prophet Alma asked his people, "Have ye received his image in your countenances? Have ye experienced this mighty change in your hearts?" (Alma 5:14). As women who live in a culture obsessed with physical appearance, it is vital for us to consider the differences between the world's version of a makeover and the Lord's version.

When *the world* makes you over, the change is temporary. Before you know it, the same world that made you over will be telling you that your hairstyle and clothing are "*so* last year" and it's time for an update. When *the Lord* makes you over, the change can be deep and lasting. King Benjamin's people claimed the Spirit had "wrought a mighty change . . . in our hearts, that we have no more disposition to do evil, but to do good continually" (Mosiah 5:2).

When *the world* makes you over, it can be expensive. Keeping up with trendy haircuts, current fashions, and the latest beauty treatments takes money. When *the Lord* makes you over, it is priceless. All He asks is that you give Him your heart, and He is especially fond of broken ones.

When *the world* makes you over, you may feel increased confidence in your social life, at school, or in the workplace. You may feel you're finally "going places." When *the Lord* makes you over, you will go places you never expected and do things you didn't think you could. He will ask you to be the Gospel Doctrine instructor or the Young Women's president or the choir director, and you will say yes, because you know "in the strength of the Lord [you can] do all things" (Alma 20:12).

When *the world* makes you over, you may look like a new person. When *the Lord* makes you over, you will actually *be* a new person.

The process of being made over spiritually is described brilliantly by C. S. Lewis:

> Imagine yourself as a living house. God comes in to rebuild that house. At first, perhaps, you can understand what He is doing. He is getting the drains right and stopping the leaks in the roof and so on: you knew that those jobs needed doing and so you are not surprised. But presently He starts knocking the house about in a way that hurts abominably and does not seem to make sense. What on earth is He up to? The explanation is that He is building quite a different house from the one you thought of—throwing out a new wing here, putting on an extra floor there, running up towers, making courtyards. You thought you were going to be made into a decent little cottage: but He is building a palace. He intends to come and live in it Himself.[4]

One aspect that inward and outward makeovers have in common is an initial analysis—determining strengths and weaknesses in order to see what changes need to be made. Concluding that a spiritual makeover was of far greater worth than any outward change, I chose to invite the Lord to be on my analysis committee, since He has revealed a foolproof method for overhauling a spirit. "And if men come unto me I will show unto them their weakness. I give unto men weakness that they may be humble; and my grace is sufficient for all men that humble themselves before me; for if they humble themselves before me, and have faith in me, then will I make weak things become strong unto them" (Ether 12:27).

Who isn't aware of their weaknesses? I've certainly felt them all of my life, but I finally dared to approach the Lord and ask Him to show them to me from *His* perspective. Fortunately, He is a merciful God and chose not to overwhelm me by revealing everything at once. Yet, in a way difficult to explain, He has begun to open the "eyes of [my] understanding" (D&C 76:19), helping me to see my innermost struggles in a new light. Seeing them clearly has enabled me to pray specifically for the help needed to peel away my most unattractive qualities.

It hasn't been pretty. In fact it has been painful and humbling, and there have been moments I've wished I never asked for help. But those times haven't lasted long, because I've begun to recognize a softening inside that only comes from making more room in my heart for the Holy Spirit. It is filling up the spaces that used to be claimed by my sins and weaknesses. Of course, my makeover won't be completed in this lifetime. It is slow work. The Lord continues to humble me as He reveals other weaknesses. I am in daily need of the Atonement. Still, this whole process of making over my spirit is fulfilling and sweet in a way I did not anticipate.

It takes courage to ask, "What could the Lord make of me if I were willing to put myself completely into His hands?" But as my heart softens, I'm more able to trust the inspired words of the scriptures that say, "the Lord looketh on the heart" (1 Samuel 16:7). By closing my eyes and mind to the damaging images of worldliness that surround me, I've experienced a growing desire to turn from the elusive fountain of youth and drink instead from "the fountain of all righteousness" (Ether 12:28).

Oh, you'll still find me at the makeup counter searching for the perfect lipstick shade—I truly believe that the Lord would not have us look unkempt—but while shadow and mascara may help my eyes to stand out, I'm more concerned that my eyes are filled with God's light. While I may fret over a bad hair day, I'm learning to care more about having a good heart day. I've come to terms with the fact that even the most expensive brand of concealer won't cover my sins and the highest quality makeup pencil can never draw "his image [on] my countenance" (Alma 5:14).

President Ezra Taft Benson said it beautifully: "The Lord works from the inside out. The world works from the outside in. The world would take the people out of the slums. Christ takes the slums out of the people. . . . The world would shape human behavior, but *Christ can change human nature*."[5]

I testify that although being made over in the Lord's image may not happen in a few hours or even years, the process can begin almost immediately as we submit our will to His and take sincere steps to invite Him into our lives so "that when he shall appear we shall be like him" (Moroni 7:48).

Notes

1 Susan W. Tanner, "The Sanctity of the Body," *Ensign*, May 2005.

2 Jeffrey R. Holland, "To Young Women," *Ensign*, May 2005.

3 Ibid.

4 C. S. Lewis, *Mere Christianity*, (New York: HarperCollins, 2001), 205.

5 Ezra Taft Benson, "Born of God," *Ensign*, November 1985, emphasis added.

CHAPTER #5
Beautiful Truths

WHEN MY OLDEST DAUGHTER, SARAH, first arrived in the Philippines as a missionary, she was assigned to an area where she was one of only a handful of Caucasians. In her first letter home, she wrote:

> I feel like a celebrity. . . . I can't go anywhere without everyone staring at me. When I say everyone, I mean EVERY SINGLE PERSON. Children that can't even be two years old come from around corners to stare at me and smile, and they call out to me, "Guwapa!!" which means "beautiful" or "pretty." *It's only because I'm white. Everyone here wishes they were white.* People shake my hand . . . and don't let go and smile at me and speak to my [native] companion in Cebuano and talk about how guwapa I am. . . . I must glow in the dark too because it doesn't matter what time of the day we're outside, everybody who is on the street [watches] me walk past.[1]

It's ironic, then, isn't it, that if I were given the chance to trade skin tones with anyone, it would be with my neighbor, Maggie, who inherited her lovely, honey-colored skin from her parents, who are natives of the Philippines. Consider the American obsession with tanning. How many millions of dollars are spent each year on tanning creams and sprays, and how many hours are spent at tanning salons, hours of life traded for a darker shade of skin because we believe it will make us more beautiful?

The more I consider what beauty really is, the more I'm convinced that there are several truths about beauty that are essential for every woman to understand:

TRUTH #1: THERE IS NO SINGLE STANDARD FOR PHYSICAL BEAUTY.

The definition of physical beauty is so subjective that every culture, even every individual, has their own ideas about the physical ideal. So when we spend enormous amounts of time and money on beauty products and procedures, exactly who are we trying to please? American pop culture is fixated on skinny females, yet many other cultures prefer women with a bit more meat on their bones. The fact that different cultures disagree about the ideal skin color and body type is proof that there isn't one true standard for physical beauty.

TRUTH #2: GOD HAS A DEFINITE STANDARD FOR SPIRITUAL BEAUTY.

In the eyes of our Heavenly Father, there is a definite standard for what constitutes real beauty. It's called purity and virtue, and it is within the reach of every woman. "The Father of lights" (James 1:17) is all about filling His children with light and truth and the Holy Spirit. Consider Parley P. Pratt's description of the ultimate beauty treatment: "The gift of the Holy Spirit . . . inspires virtue, kindness, goodness, tenderness, gentleness, and charity. *It develops beauty of person, form and features*. . . . It is, as it were, marrow to the bone, joy to the heart, light to the eyes, music to the ears, and life to the whole being."[2]

President Gordon B. Hinckley describes beauty this way: "Of all the creations of the Almighty, there is none more beautiful, none more inspiring than a lovely daughter of God who walks in virtue with an understanding of why she should do so, who honors and respects her body as a thing sacred and divine, who cultivates her mind and constantly enlarges the horizon of her understanding, who nurtures her spirit with everlasting truth."[3]

TRUTH #3: WE BECOME CONFUSED ABOUT THE MEANING OF BEAUTY WHEN WE GET OUR INFORMATION FROM CONFLICTING SOURCES.

Recently, I did an unofficial study with the intent to determine why women are so confused about what beauty really is. My research began in the magazine section at Walmart. I opened several women's and teen magazines and skimmed the table of contents. Here are some of the titles of the articles inside:

"The Most Beautiful Woman in the World (And 95 Other Fabulous Faces)"

"9 Beauty Tricks That'll Amp up Your Sex Appeal Instantly"
"How to Get That Hollywood Look"
"I Hate My Hair"
"How to Step up Your Sex Appeal: 10 Easy Ways"
The second phase of my highly scientific research took place in my family room. Picking a stack of Church magazines from the table by my sofa, I glanced through the contents and found long lists of articles I would not be ashamed to read even if my mother were looking over my shoulder:
"A Return to Virtue"
"The Potter and the Clay (Allowing God to Shape Our Lives Brings True Happiness)"
"Let Virtue Garnish Your Thoughts"
"Daughters of God"
"The Transforming Power of Faith and Character"
The official results of my unofficial study: we're getting our information from conflicting sources. No wonder we're confused about what constitutes true beauty and what's expected of covenant women. Poring over glossy magazine photos of celebrity faces will always foster insecurities but isn't likely to inspire us to be more virtuous—why torture ourselves? I testify that the truth will make us free, but eternal truths are rarely found in glamour magazines, torrid romance novels, television shows and commercials, blockbuster movies, or much other modern media. If worldly magazines currently coexist with the *Ensign* on our end tables, we need to rethink that situation. If we're watching movies that leave us discouraged about ourselves and self-critical because we don't measure up to the unattainable looks of the leading lady, those feelings should be a clue that we need to change our viewing habits.

Distancing ourselves from the constant barrage of images the world parades before us can significantly lessen the pressure we feel to look and act according to worldly standards. We might even have to distance ourselves from friends who are obsessed with physical beauty, particularly if they're trying to achieve it through extreme measures. These are tough choices, but the benefit is a healthier attitude about our own appearance.

TRUTH #4: EARTH LIFE IS LIKE A MASQUERADE BALL.

The truth is (drum roll, please) earth life is an awful lot like a masquerade ball where costumes and masks are provided by the host, who has carefully selected them for each guest. A few of those who attend receive costumes that are gorgeous in both detail and design. Others are given costumes that appear to be ill-fitting, seriously damaged, or even incomplete. The vast majority of the costumes fall somewhere between these two extremes. It is easy for us, as guests, to become preoccupied with comparing our costume to others', making little attempt to see beyond the façade and determine who is really behind each mask. Oddly enough, we rarely even catch a glimpse of our own true selves because we can't get past the costume we see in the mirror.

Won't we be surprised on the day when costumes are cast aside and we discover there is little beauty in some of the people whose costumes we have envied, and even more surprisingly, some of the spirits who wore the least desirable costumes on earth are glorious beyond description.

TRUTH #5: THE PROCESS OF AGING IS PART OF HEAVENLY FATHER'S PLAN FOR HIS CHILDREN.

Continuing the masquerade comparison, even the most elegant and admired costumes at the ball eventually wrinkle and become worn and faded. This happens despite concerted efforts to iron and mend the trouble spots. Every costume changes over time, so if our self-esteem is based on our appearance, we may experience serious emotional struggles when we discover that first gray hair or detect lines on our once-smooth skin.

When it comes to worldly beauty, public enemy number one is aging—as if growing older was an unnatural occurrence. I have thought long and hard on this subject—as I suspect most women do when facing middle age. The Spirit has reminded me on several occasions that the process of aging is an integral part of Heavenly Father's plan, and if we approach this phenomenon from an eternal perspective, aging will teach us significant lessons.

Contrary to popular belief, aging is not a tragedy. The true tragedy occurs when we reach a stage of life when our wisdom and experience could be a tremendous blessing to others but we're so caught up with frantic attempts to look younger that we miss opportunities to serve.

I adore the following passage on middle age from Anne Morrow Lindbergh:

> We Americans, with our terrific emphasis on youth . . . tend to belittle the afternoon of life and even to pretend it never comes. We push the clock back and try to prolong the morning, overreaching and overstraining ourselves in the unnatural effort. . . . In our breathless attempts, we often miss the flowering that waits for afternoon.
>
> For is it not possible that middle age can be looked upon as a period of second flowering, second growth, even a kind of second adolescence? It is true that society in general does not help one accept this interpretation of the second half of life. And therefore this period of expanding is often tragically misunderstood.
>
> Many people never climb above the plateau of forty-to-fifty. The signs that presage growth, so similar, it seems to me, to those in early adolescence: discontent, restlessness, doubt, despair, longing, are interpreted falsely as signs of decay. In youth one does not as often misinterpret the signs; one accepts them quite rightly, as growing pains. One takes them seriously, listens to them, follows where they lead.
>
> But in middle age, because of the false assumption that it is a period of decline, one interprets these life-signs paradoxically, as signs of approaching death. . . . Anything, rather than stand still and learn from them. One tries to cure the signs of growth, to exorcise them, as if they were devils, when really they might be angels of annunciation . . . of a new stage of living.[4]

It is interesting to note that these words were first published more than fifty years ago.

A retirement community was built near my neighborhood for residents fifty-five years of age and older, and many of the homes are within the boundaries of my ward. What a blessing it has been to watch the new residents move in, both couples and singles. These are some of the finest people I've met. The women in particular have been an inspiration to me. They are lovely in every way—their faces radiating goodness earned from years of service and sacrifice, patience and empathy learned from personal trials, and the wisdom and good humor that only decades of life experience can bring.

TRUTH #6: THE LORD CAN HELP US OVERCOME OUR NEGATIVE FEELINGS ABOUT OUR BODIES.

But what if we truly despise our body or we're afraid to age? Perhaps we even have serious physical deformities that contribute to our poor self-image. Must we simply endure these negative feelings until the Resurrection? Of course we're deeply grateful that Jesus Christ has blessed us with the hope of a perfect body someday, but most of the time "someday" feels impossibly far away. What then?

Let me share with you something lovely I came across some months ago. I was deeply touched as I read the following account from Sister Merrilee Boyack. Her message is powerful and potentially healing for anyone who deals with deep-seated issues about their appearance—and isn't that most of us?

> I have spent my entire lifetime feeling unattractive. . . . So you can imagine how I felt when I was diagnosed with breast cancer and told that I had to have a mastectomy. You've GOT to be kidding me. Wasn't I ugly enough? The thought of losing my hair, which I felt was my one saving grace, hit me. I shall never forget the day when . . . I realized that by the end of the month I would be bald. Bald. Ugly. Could I survive all this emotionally? On that day I prayed to Heavenly Father and asked for a gift. I asked for the gift of healing of my feelings about my appearance. . . . I knew this was not something I could survive very well emotionally on my own. And I was tired of feeling ugly for fifty years of my life. I wanted healing. And I knew the only way to get it was to get it from God. So I asked.
>
> Now a strange thing began to happen. Day after day I felt prettier. I know that is very strange and hard

to explain. I began to notice things about myself that I liked and were attractive.

And then came the day . . . when my hair was going. . . . [My son] came home on his lunch hour. I buzzed his hair, and then he buzzed mine. As he was buzzing it, he commented, "It's not every day you get to buzz off your mother's hair!"

And then came the time to face the mirror. And an amazing thing happened. I looked in that mirror and saw beauty. My eyes that I had always hated were shining. My skin was glowing. I had a good head! And a big smile. I realized that I was truly beautiful.

I told my husband that I have felt more beautiful in the last two months than I have ever felt in my life. He laughed and said it must have been the hair! But I know something deeper has happened. God has healed my feelings about my appearance. I have finally been able to see myself as He sees me—a marvelous work of art. And the voices that I have carried in my head for decades have been completely silenced. It was a gift from Him—pure and simple.

I have learned a deep lesson. God creates beauty. It is that simple. And when He created me, He created a lovely, pretty, downright CUTE daughter. I have also realized that every single one of us is beautiful. Yeah, yeah, we have inner beauty. But I have discovered that every single one of us in all our shapes and sizes and ages and conditions, are truly beautiful on the *outside*. That was something I had not understood until now."[5]

One particular line from Sister Boyack has echoed through my mind since reading her story: *God has healed my feelings about my appearance.* If issues about our physical appearance are undermining our confidence and making it difficult for us to believe that we are of worth, then it's high time we address this sensitive subject with the One who created us. Imagine how liberating it would be to leave our negative feelings behind, freeing our spirits to actively pursue the kind of life God intends for His daughters. Imagine, in place of self-consciousness and self-loathing, a life of service and sanctification.

TRUTH #7: PHYSICAL BEAUTY IS NOT A REQUIREMENT FOR SPIRITUAL PERFECTION. (HALLELUJAH!)

If we need scriptural evidence that God isn't fretting over our physical appearance, try this: referring to the Savior, the prophet Isaiah wrote, "He hath no form nor comeliness; and when we shall see him, there is no beauty that we should desire him" (Isaiah 53:2). That ought to give us something to chew on. Apparently, even Jesus Himself didn't possess an extraordinary share of good looks, and yet we sing about our "Beautiful Savior."

Meaning what? Meaning, the Savior was able to achieve perfection without being considered particularly attractive, so the type of perfection we're asked to strive for has nothing to do with physical beauty. We're asked to keep our bodies clean and healthy and modestly covered, but nowhere in the scriptures are we given a description of the ideal hair color, skin tone, or body size—*because there is none.* The phrase "perfect size six" is not found in the standard works. (Unless it's buried in Leviticus—I suppose I could have missed it in there.)

What *do* the scriptures say about our bodies? "I am fearfully and wonderfully made" (Psalm 139:14). Squinting into the mirror first thing in the morning, we can sort of understand the fearful part. But honestly, do we believe that we are *fearfully* and *wonderfully* made? Can we trust that the God who created man and woman in His own image knew what He was doing? Heavenly Father has a plan of salvation for each of us, and the particular body we were given is an integral part of that plan. Through our bodies we will be tempted and frustrated and humbled. As we learn to respect these sacred temples and allow our spirits to control them, our bodies will enable us to experience a higher level of joy than our spirits alone can achieve. As stated by Elder David A. Bednar, "Our physical bodies make possible a breadth, a depth, and an intensity of experience that simply could not be obtained in our premortal estate."[6]

TRUTH #8: YOU ARE BEAUTIFUL.

Yes, I'm talking to *you.* Don't roll your eyes or sigh. It's time we "get over ourselves"—even with all of our perceived imperfections—and stop the negative self-talk. If you still need help in this area of your life, please refer back to Truth #6. I pray the day will come for all of us when we can be at peace with our appearance. Then we will finally be free to shift our focus more fully to Christ.

Notes

1 Sarah Christofferson, personal correspondence, August 2010.
2 Parley P. Pratt, "Key to the Science of Theology," 101–102, emphasis added.
3 Gordon B. Hinckley, "Our Responsibility to Our Young Women," *Ensign*, September 1988.
4 Anne Morrow Lindbergh, *Gift from the Sea*, (New York: Pantheon Books, a division of Random House, 2005), 78–80.
5 Merrilee Brown Boyack, Time Out For Women Blog, February 2009.
6 David A. Bednar, "Things As They Really Are," CES Fireside, May 2009.

CHAPTER #6
Sending Signals

WARNING: ANYONE NOT UP TO some straight talk on a touchy subject should skip to the next chapter. Seriously.

Okay, since when did looking "sexy" become such an intense focus for millions of modern women? I have read every page of the standard works, but never once have I run across the admonition to be sexy. You can find the terms "carnal" and "sensual" in the scriptures, but isn't it interesting that they're generally paired with the word "devilish." Nowhere in the teachings of Jesus Christ—or Isaiah or Nephi for that matter—is there any indication that trying to be sexy should be a woman's priority. "We believe in being honest, true, chaste, benevolent, virtuous" (Article of Faith 1:13) and a whole lot of other things, but sexy has never been on that list.

According to my trusty dictionary, the word *sexy* means "arousing sexual desire or interest." May I be so bold as to suggest that since, in the Lord's plan of happiness, sexual intimacy is reserved for marriage, then it follows that "sexy" is something strictly between a wife and her husband. Suggestive dress and attitudes have no business in the workplace, the restaurant, the mall, the yard, the gym, or any other public setting. Yet we frequently see females of many ages—sometimes even in a religious setting—dressed in a way calculated to draw attention to their bodies. Many of these women don't know better, but, Sisters, *we do*—or at least we should.

Admittedly, those of us who have figures considered to be somewhat less than the cultural ideal rarely suffer from serious temptation to display cellulite, stretch marks, or spider veins. Our hearts go out to those blessed with more glorious physical tabernacles. We feel for you. (Okay, that may be stretching it a bit . . .) Still, we can *imagine* that the temptation to show off a lovely physique must be strong. But I've yet to meet the woman, no matter how attractive, who appreciates another female parading sexy dress or attitudes around her husband, fiancé, boyfriend, brothers, nephews, or sons.

While we're being completely honest here, let's not forget that no self-respecting husband, fiancé, or boyfriend wants their significant other intentionally turning another man's head. Any woman purposely seeking another man's attention in order to make her husband jealous is playing a very dangerous game. In chapter 31 of Proverbs, the question is asked, "Who can find a virtuous woman?" The verses that follow list the qualities of such a woman. (See Proverbs 31:10–31.) Want to hear the very first one? "The heart of her husband doth safely trust in her" (v. 11). Could there be a deeper compliment than that?

Sisters, this is serious business. Do we really think we won't be held accountable if we dress or act with the intent to arouse sexual desire or awareness in anyone outside of marriage? In 2005, Elder Dallin H. Oaks gave an address about the evils of pornography, wherein he made this powerful statement: "Young women, please understand that if you dress immodestly, you are magnifying this problem by becoming pornography to some of the men who see you."[1] Elder Oaks could not have stated it more clearly. The men of these high-tech latter days are fighting a tough battle to keep their thoughts pure. Why would we want to make it harder for them than it already is?

Does this mean we must go about makeup free, wearing sackcloth and ashes? Good grief! Of course not. While immodest women aren't likely to bring people to Christ, neither are prudish, unkempt drudges. Remember, "If there is anything virtuous, lovely, or of good report or praiseworthy, we seek after these things" (Articles of Faith 1:13). There's nothing wrong with trying to be attractive, but if our goal is to look "hot" in public, there's a problem. *Hot* suggests that we're seeking an inappropriate kind of attention.

I would bet that most of us have, within our circle of acquaintance, women who have a true grasp of what modesty means. Observe them closely. They are clean, classy, and attractive, as well as intelligent and articulate. Because their modest dress and behavior are "an outward expression of an inward commitment,"[2] these women command respect wherever they go.

While pondering the importance of modesty one morning, my mind reached clear back to something I learned during grade school. I remembered studying Native American cultures. In addition to their spoken languages, many tribes used an interesting form of nonverbal communication: smoke signals. By sending up separate puffs of smoke from a fire, it was possible to get a simple message to an individual or group—even from a distance. In a similar manner, the way we dress and act sends definite signals to those around us. "What you put on your body 'talks,' and everyone who sees you 'hears' what you are saying."[3]

Consider what type of signals we send when we choose to wear tight-fitting clothing. In the age of spandex, we might benefit from a reminder that wearing a skintight outfit can be nearly as revealing as exposing skin. I am *not* suggesting we buy a baggy, shapeless wardrobe, but if we look like we've been shrink-wrapped into our clothing, we ought to examine our motives and rethink our choices.

More food for thought: two women with different body types could try on the same outfit with widely varying results. Those with more voluptuous figures will likely have to go to greater lengths to be modest. A modest woman, no matter what her shape is, is careful to draw attention to her eyes and face. This means avoiding clothing which, either by cut or strategically placed ornamentation, is designed to attract the eye to specific parts of the body. I recall the first time I saw a young woman with the word *cheerleader* emblazoned across the seat of her sweatpants. Guess where the eyes of everyone at her high school were drawn that day? Hopefully, that's not the kind of attention we want.

You know what? This is not a comfortable subject for me to write about. I'm no more qualified to speak out on modesty than the next woman, but I have felt compelled to do so. It's not my intent to judge or point fingers—only to encourage an attitude check of sorts. Believe me, pondering this topic has caused me to take a hard look at myself and my motives. I have learned that modest dress and behavior allow me a sense of freedom from self-consciousness. When

I'm not preoccupied with having to tug continually at my neckline or hemline, I am able to give my complete attention to those with whom I interact.

I think of a conversation I once had with a friend. She told of being at the local swimming pool with her teenage daughters and coming face to face with their Young Women leader—who was wearing a skimpy bikini. Talk about awkward! The leader was visibly embarrassed. As my friend and her girls slipped into their car to leave, one of the daughters burst into tears. She was disappointed and confused. Were all those Young Women lessons about high standards and modesty just hot air? How could she trust again in what her leader told her? Without even breathing a word, that leader sent a powerful message.

This story reminds me of a personal experience. I once sat in a congregation of young women who had gathered for a fireside. The main speaker, a Church member who had recently won a beauty pageant, was poised and confident as she delivered her message. Unfortunately, no one in that gathering will remember a single word she spoke. I vividly recall the audible gasp that went up from the audience when she turned from the podium to her seat, and we were all treated to a view of her bare back. Her dress, though perfectly modest in the front, was cut out behind from neckline to waistline. Yes, she sent a definite message that evening—but it wasn't the one she had intended.

My point in sharing these stories is not to pass judgment but merely to demonstrate that what we choose to wear makes an impact on the people around us. In *For the Strength of Youth*, the Church has set forth basic guidelines: "Immodest clothing is any clothing that is tight, sheer, or revealing in any other manner. Young women should avoid short shorts and short skirts, shirts that do not cover the stomach, and clothing that does not cover the shoulders or is low-cut in the front or the back."

Women who have received their temple endowment have the privilege of wearing the temple garments. Some have complained because the garments are often not compatible with the fashions of the world. But isn't that exactly the point? Part of the purpose of wearing them is to remind us of the covenants we have made and to help us live the Lord's standard of modesty. Sister Linda S. Reeves has said, "There are . . . great blessings and protecting promises associated with the proper wearing of our temple garments. . . . I testify, sisters, that when we strive to wear the garment properly, our Father recognizes it as a great sign of our love and devotion to Him. It is a sign of the covenant we have made with Him." If we resist wearing the garments or wear them improperly, we have not fully understood the blessings and protection they provide.

The principle of modesty encompasses much more than just covering skin. It involves every aspect of our appearance and even our manner of speech and behavior. According to Sister Sylvia Allred, the degree to which we practice true modesty "demonstrates our understanding of the gospel of Jesus Christ."[4] One oft-overlooked facet of this principle is the importance of avoiding extremes in makeup, nails, hairstyle, hair color, accessories, fashion, piercings, tattoos, and anything used to make us stand out but not to stand for Christ.

As mentioned in the first chapter of this book, the prophet Isaiah wrote about wimples and crisping pins (see Isaiah 3:22). Later, Nephi spoke of "silks, and scarlets, and fine-twined linens" (1 Nephi 13:7). It's all the same sort of thing, isn't it? Many of us women seem inclined to ornament our bodies in one way or another. I wonder which of Eve's granddaughters was the first to make a daisy chain to accessorize her coat of skins (see Moses 4:27).

I am not condemning simple, tasteful attempts to look attractive, but when we claim to be Christians, we must take care that our outward adornment never overshadows Christ's image in our countenance. (See Alma 5:14.)

After witnessing a trend toward multiple ear and body piercings and the increasing popularity of tattoos, our Church leaders released an official statement: The First Presidency and the Council of the Twelve have taken the position that the Church discourages tattoos. It also discourages "the piercing of the body for other than medical purposes," although it takes no position "on the minimal piercing of the ears by women for one pair of earrings."[5]

Referring to this statement, Elder D. Todd Christofferson asks an important question: "Why would the Prophet of God talk about things so seemingly insignificant? Because they are not insignificant. Defiling or defacing God's creation, His temple, makes a mock of that which is sacred. This can be perceived as insignificant only to one who has lost a sense of the sacred."[6]

In July 2010, my brother, John, "kidnapped" me for my birthday, flying me to San Francisco, where we spent several days exploring. Knowing how much I enjoy visiting art museums, John had purchased tickets to the M. H. de Young Memorial Museum, where we saw—on loan from the Musee d'Orsay in Paris—the original painting "Arrangement in Grey and Black No. 1," better known as "Whistler's Mother." As we stood viewing this famous work, I couldn't help but wonder what an ordeal it must have been to acquire permission to have it transported across an ocean, what an exorbitant sum of money must have been paid to insure it, and what it was costing to hire the security detail which guarded it. If we humans take such extreme care of what we consider to be a masterpiece, should we not show the same kind of respect for our bodies—the greatest of all our Heavenly Father's creations?

Must we always wait for the prophet to make a specific declaration about each part of our dress and behavior before we will make necessary changes to be more authentic witnesses of the Savior? Or can we be honest enough—mature enough—to admit that certain ways of dressing and adorning ourselves mark us clearly as followers of the world and not of Jesus Christ?

When we choose to be extreme in any facet of our appearance, we are sending inappropriate signals just as surely as if we were sporting low necklines and skintight apparel. We are making a cry for attention. My husband once told me of a young woman he interviewed to work as a clerk in the accounting department of his office. She appeared to be clean cut, conservative, and qualified for the position, so she was hired.

Imagine the surprise of the management team when, soon after starting her job, this young lady began to show up for work with multiple tattoos exposed, as well as several rings in her nose and lips—tattoos and jewelry which she had hidden or removed before. She was unhappy when her supervisor reminded her that she was hired partially because her conservative appearance reflected the values of the company. By sporting more extreme styles, she no longer accurately represented that company.

How will we lead other souls to Christ if we do not represent Him outwardly as well as spiritually? *The people we associate with can tell just by looking at us whether we're trying to please the Lord or the world.*

I wish to emphasize that those who choose to be extreme in their dress and appearance should not automatically be judged as bad or evil. We should be so busy trying to become like Christ that we don't have time to waste judging other people. But as members of the Church we must be aware, as Elder Robert D. Hales has emphasized, that "when we make and keep covenants, we are coming out of the world and into the Kingdom of God. Our appearance should reflect that. . . . Ultimately, how we dress will greatly influence our obedience to commandments and our devotion to covenants."[7]

When we're teaching a Primary class, a group of young women, or our family at home, the lesson could be about charity or faith or a dozen other gospel topics. Yet *every time* we're with our daughters, our nieces, or any girl within our circle of influence, we're also teaching a nonverbal lesson on modesty, and *we* are the visual aid. There's no escaping the fact that what we wear to church, the grocery store, the park, or the pool is sending signals to everyone around us.

Here's a simple list of questions to help determine where we stand on the principle of modesty:

* When choosing what to wear, is it my intent to show as much skin as possible, while just barely covering my temple garments? Do I ever remove, pin, or alter those garments in order to accommodate today's fashions?

* Is my clothing so tight that it looks like I've been shrink-wrapped?

* Am I able to sit down, bend over, or raise my arms without embarrassing the people around me or drawing inappropriate attention to my body?

* If I were to run into my bishop unexpectedly today, would either he or I be embarrassed about what I'm wearing?

* Have I delayed receiving my temple endowment simply because I don't want the temple garments to restrict my choice of clothing?

* Who am I trying to impress by the way I dress? What kind of signals am I trying to send to the people around me?

If this is an area where we struggle, perhaps we have not yet experienced an awakening as to who we really are. I know of no surer way to receive this testimony than to ask for it—to search and ponder and then humbly kneel and plead with Heavenly Father for a sense of our divine nature, petitioning for help in viewing ourselves and everyone around us as children of God. When that understanding comes to us, we will be eager to show the young women and girls in our lives how to dress and act like the godly women we are meant to be.

To those women who are already shining examples of beautifully modest living, I applaud you. I am deeply grateful for the influence you have had on my sons and daughters and for inspiring me to try to emulate your behavior. I also applaud the men, young and old, who honor, respect, and encourage the efforts of modest women.

Even if we don't fully understand the reason that slight changes to our wardrobe make a difference, we will be blessed as we strive to obey the principle of modesty. The following statement from President Ezra Taft Benson is well worth memorizing: "When obedience ceases to be an irritant and becomes our quest, in that moment God will endow us with power."[8] I testify that the day we stop making excuses to justify immodesty in our lives and commit instead to embracing and obeying the Lord's standards, we'll be on our way to becoming powerful instruments for good at a time when our influence is desperately needed.

Notes

1 Dallin H. Oaks, "Pornography," *Ensign*, May 2005, 87, emphasis added.
2 Carlos E. Asay, "The Temple Garment: An Outward Expression of an Inward Commitment, *Ensign*, August 1997.
3 Q&A: Questions and Answers, *New Era*, January 2004, 16.
4 Sylvia A. Allred, "Modesty: A Timeless Principle for All," *Liahona*, July 2009.
5 Gordon B. Hinckley, "Great Shall Be the Peace of Thy Children," *Ensign*, November 2000.

6 D. Todd Christofferson, "A Sense of the Sacred," speeches.byu.edu, November 7, 2004.

7 Robert D. Hales, "Modesty: Reverence for the Lord," *Liahona*, August 2008.

8 Ezra Taft Benson, in Donald L. Staheli, "Obedience—Life's Great Challenge," *Ensign*, May 1998, 82.

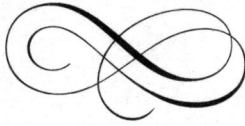

Section Three
SHIELDING OUR SPIRITS

CHAPTER #7
The Parable of the Bathtub

It's one of those rare evenings—nobody else around, no meetings to attend. You're caught up on your laundry and current church assignments (total fantasy, of course). After standing on your feet most of the day, you're craving a warm, relaxing bath. You start the water running in the tub, making sure it's good and hot because you intend to soak for a full hour. Suddenly the phone rings. Habit propels you into the next room, where a glance at the caller ID tells you that *this* call cannot be ignored.

Ten minutes later, you're congratulating yourself on keeping the conversation short, when you remember the running water. You dash back to the bathroom, frantically turning the knobs of the faucet. Whew! The nearly overflowing tub is just waiting for you. But there's a problem. You notice steam rising and realize that the water is scalding hot. The tub is full, so adding cold water is not an option. Neither is plunging your arm in to release the plug and drain a bit out. You decide to wait five minutes. Surely by then the bath will have cooled enough that you won't be risking serious burns. The seconds crawl by. Your aching muscles are crying out for a soak and will not be silenced.

So . . . you dip one foot in the water. *Aaugh!* It's painfully hot! How about the tip of one toe? In and out quickly, again and again. Then more toes. The process is tedious but worth it because now you've got a whole foot in the water, and the delicious warmth is spreading. It takes several minutes more to ease in all the way, but it's sooo heavenly. You wish you had time to make this a nightly ritual. A quarter of an hour later, you're beginning to doze when you gradually become aware that the water has cooled noticeably. Drowsily, you drain a bit out and reach for the faucet, turning on a thin stream of steaming water to make yourself comfortably warm.

The moral of this story? She who eases into evil will find herself in hot water.

What a startling phenomenon. Had you jumped into the burning tub when you first saw it was full, you would have screamed and scrambled out immediately, likely in tears. But toe by toe by foot by leg you were able to enter the water—even finding it soothing. Soon, you found that you needed more of the hot stuff to maintain the desired temperature.

The spiritual application is obvious. It is crucial that we recognize areas where we may already have a toe or foot in spiritually dangerous waters. The descent into evil can be so gradual as to be nearly imperceptible. Satan is no fool. He doesn't tempt with shock treatments. Rather, he patiently persuades us by degrees until we find ourselves firmly in his territory, "and thus the devil cheateth [our] souls, and leadeth [us] away carefully down to hell" (2 Nephi 28:21).

How often have we heard or said, "It was such a great movie—*except for that one scene?*" For some unaccountable reason, we assume that spiritual poison is acceptable in small doses, while we wouldn't dream of ingesting insecticide or motor oil—not even a spoonful. What if we collected all those seemingly insignificant scenes, spliced them together, and watched them as a full-length film? No doubt we would be horrified and offended. Yet, one questionable scene at a time, we become desensitized to the evil right under our nose. We forget that in the long run, the effects of being poisoned by degrees can be just as deadly as a single heavy dose.

One of the greatest dangers we face in these high-tech latter days is the threat of becoming desensitized to the whisperings of the Holy Spirit. Once this occurs, it is just a matter of time before we begin easing into evil. Speaking to a group of Nephites, the prophet Jacob described some of the women this way: their "feelings are exceedingly tender and chaste and delicate . . . which thing is pleasing unto God" (Jacob 2:7). Though words like *tender* and *delicate* might describe something fragile, we must not equate them with weakness. Jacob was referring to pure minds and fine-tuned spirits—the kind that operate on the same frequency as the Holy Ghost—that enabled these Nephite women to discern His promptings. Make no mistake; any woman in possession of these qualities has access to tremendous spiritual power.

We become desensitized to the gentle whispers of the Spirit when we allow ourselves to be overexposed to all that is loud, intense, and fast-paced. I go to the movies only a couple of times each year, mostly because it's difficult to find a show which aligns with my values. But there's another reason I hesitate to go—it's the "in your face" previews shown before the feature film. After the visual and aural assault of four or five previews for movies I'd never dream of watching, I feel like I've whooshed down the steepest rollercoaster drop of my life, but in this case, the 100-mph stomach-shivering thrill lasts for ten minutes instead of ten seconds. It's just too intense. I've tried closing my eyes and covering my ears, but the vibrations alone are powerful enough to cause an adrenaline rush. Frequent exposure to these kinds of thrills can be damaging to our spirits.

I never leave the temple feeling like someone stuffed my spirit in a blender and hit the pulverize button, but that is exactly the sensation I've experienced in many a movie theater. We're exposed to sensory overload for an alarmingly high percentage of our waking hours, saturated with sound waves and visual stimulation. Have you ever attended a concert that left your ears ringing for days afterward? What about that super-sized fast-food combo you wolfed down for lunch yesterday? It was loaded with sweeteners and sodium to boost the flavor, and with more calories and fat grams than a body needs in an entire day.

If we've become accustomed to super-sized meals, highly caffeinated energy drinks, the repeated adrenaline rush of violent movies or extreme sports, or the constant noise of our iPods, we shouldn't be surprised when it's nearly impossible to hear the promptings of the still small voice. How can the Spirit compete with all of the noise and stimulants? *He doesn't even try.* He will not increase His volume to a shout. So how do we protect ourselves from spiritual desensitization?

I recall, as a young missionary, being informed that on the next preparation day, our whole mission would participate in a "Book of Mormon Marathon." We were to rise early that morning to take care of essential laundry and letters, and then gather, fasting, with other missionaries in our zone and read the Book of Mormon until dinnertime, when we would pray together and end our fast. Now, I love reading the scriptures, but I confess to being less than enthusiastic to fast on a P-day and to give up the chance to unwind a bit.

Despite my poor attitude, I chose to obey. On the appointed day, in the designated location, I opened my scriptures to begin reading. At that time my personal study was in the late chapters of Alma, which are filled with accounts of the nearly nonstop wars between the Nephites and the Lamanites. To me, this was not the most meaningful part of the book—not by a long shot. I debated whether to skip to a more riveting section but finally chose to just plow through the "battle stuff" in record time.

Perhaps it was the fasting or maybe it was reading for several hours straight, but as I made my way through chapters I'd read many times previously, I began to see the account in a new light. By the time I reached chapter 50, I was engrossed in the story. A line from verse one seemed to stand out in bold letters: **Moroni did not stop making preparations for war.** Even in times of peace, this righteous Nephite captain took steps to ensure the safety of his people. Moroni directed his armies to build layers of protection.

First, they dug up heaps of earth "round about all the cities" (Alma 50:1). Next, works of timbers (fences) were built. The third layer was a frame of pickets on top of the timbers. Then Moroni erected towers that overlooked those pickets and built places of security on those towers. The Nephites were also prepared to cast stones down on anyone who approached. These layers of outward protection were added to the breastplates and head-plates, the arm-shields and thick clothing which Moroni had already issued to each of his men (see Alma 43:19 and 49:24).

As a result of the Nephites' efforts, when the Lamanites came to battle at the city of Ammonihah, "because [they] had destroyed it once because of the iniquity of the people, they supposed it would again become an easy prey for them. . . . But behold, how great was their disappointment. . . . The chief captains . . . were astonished exceedingly, because of the wisdom of the Nephites in preparing their places of security"; a city "which had hitherto been a weak place, had now . . . become strong." (See Alma 49:3–5, 14.)

What spiritual parallels exist for these layers of protection? I believe that prayer is our first line of defense—true communication with our Heavenly Father, requesting His help in discerning good from evil, especially when the difference is subtle. Intense study of the scriptures and the words of modern-day prophets must be the next layer. No surprise here. These are sources of powerful truths and warnings which assist us in discovering patterns of wickedness so we may avoid them.

The *order* of other layers may be subject to debate, but the list certainly includes obedience, repentance, fasting, temple worship, pondering, modesty, paying a full tithe, living the law of chastity, honesty, partaking of the sacrament worthily, keeping the Word of Wisdom, and maintaining purity of thought. The list could continue for pages. Every sincere prayer we offer, every moment we search the scriptures, every act of obedience to God is an invitation to the Holy Spirit to participate more fully in our lives, and increases our ability to recognize His promptings. *That* is the ultimate protection.

Since childhood I've been fascinated with the prophet Lehi's vision of the tree of life, with its many symbols. We read of a path that leads to a glorious tree, "whose fruit [is] desirable to make one happy" (1 Nephi 8:10). We're also introduced to various distractions and roadblocks which can prevent us from reaching the tree. Lehi's determination to lead his family to taste the sweetness of the fruit shows us how intense our focus must be if we want to avoid the things that desensitize our spirits and prevent us from tasting that sweetness ourselves.

Pondering the value of having a single-minded focus on a goal brings to my mind an incident which occurred decades ago. My oldest brother, Steve, and I were touring several Asian countries with a group of university students. First stop: Japan. On a Sunday morning, as the group boarded a crowded subway, Steve found a seat a bit away from his friends. The motion of the train, combined with jet lag, lulled him into a sound sleep. In fact, he slept so deeply that he was completely oblivious when his group reached its destination and exited the subway.

Blissfully unaware of their departure, my snoozing brother continued his journey out of Tokyo—*way* out of Tokyo. He finally awoke when a subway janitor brushed a broom against Steve's shoe. Looking around, he found that he was sitting on a deserted subway car, having reached the end of the line. Instead of a bustling city around him, there were only empty fields. Back in downtown Tokyo the subway signs had romanizations under the Japanese kanjis (symbols) so even those who didn't speak Japanese could read and understand, but Steve was now so far out of the city that the signs had *only* kanjis, which he could not read. He had no way of even knowing the name of the place he had reached, and he didn't have his passport with him. An attempt to use a pay phone only brought frustration since the Japanese operator spoke no English. What does one do in such a pre–cell phone predicament? How does someone so lost reach their destination?

While a dozen thoughts and prayers rushed through his mind, Steve spotted a blonde head among the few dark-haired people on the subway platform, and he approached its owner, hoping she could speak English and help him. Bingo. The blonde woman was an American, working in Japan as an English teacher. She kindly identified the symbols for Tokyo for Steve and even copied them onto his hand in ink. After steering him in the right direction, she encouraged him to keep looking for the same kanjis on the subway signs and follow them till he arrived back in Tokyo. Telling him that one symbol stood for *to* and the other for *kyo*, she cautioned him against switching the order or he would end up in Kyoto, hundreds of miles from where he wanted to be.

Fortunately, Steve was carrying enough money in his wallet to purchase tickets for the ride back to Tokyo. There was no napping on *this* journey, no casual approach to finding his way. The first order of business, he discovered, was to preserve the two ink symbols on the palm of his hand since the combination of heat, humidity, and nervous perspiration were threatening to melt them away. Palm up and flat, he studied the symbols closely, looking for corresponding kanjis on subway signs. Occasionally, he had to get the attention of a Japanese traveler, point to his hand, and say, "Tokyo," so people could help him find the correct symbols. Many hours later, Steve arrived in downtown Tokyo, taking a cab for the final leg of the journey to the Miyako Hotel, where his university group—especially his sister—was greatly relieved to see him again.

By identifying the symbols to follow and keeping a single-minded focus on his intended goal, Steve made it safely back to Tokyo. In order to reach the tree of life and partake of its fruit, we must be focused on our goal with the same intensity.

If we think we can casually saunter up the strait and narrow path and make it to the tree, we deceive ourselves. If we believe we can keep one foot on the path while dangling the other in the river of filthy water, think again. Let's be honest, anyone knowingly dangling a foot in filthy water has already left the path. Fence-sitting is never comfortable—sooner or later we will land on one side or the other, and it is usually the path of least resistance not the strait and narrow.

Asking ourselves the following questions, posed by Sister Elaine S. Dalton, may help us determine where we are in relation to the path: "Could it be that we have been slowly desensitized into thinking that high moral standards are old fashioned and not relevant or important in today's society? . . . Could it be that first we tolerate then accept, and eventually embrace the vice that surrounds us? Could it be that we have been deceived by false role models and persuasive media messages that cause us to forget our divine identity? Are we . . . being poisoned by degrees?"[1]

One part of Lehi's vision haunts me. We read of people who pressed forward on the path, clinging to the rod of iron, who reached the tree and partook of the fruit, but "after they had partaken of the fruit of the tree they did cast their eyes about as if they were ashamed" (1 Nephi 8:24) because they saw other people mocking them. In shifting their focus away from the tree of life, they "fell away into forbidden paths and were lost" (1 Nephi 8:28). Nephi and Lehi had the right idea. Concerning those who were pointing the finger of scorn, Nephi's words were short and sweet: "We heeded them not" (1 Nephi 8:33).

As we follow Captain Moroni's example, erecting layers of protection around ourselves, we will be able to keep our focus on the tree of life and avoid the trap of easing into evil—thus keeping ourselves out of hot water.

———————————

Notes

1 Elaine S. Dalton, "A Return to Virtue," *Ensign*, November 2008.

CHAPTER #8
Virtual Life or Virtuous Life

FOR THE FIRST TWO YEARS of her life, my daughter, Rebecca, didn't seem to require sleep. Much of that time is a blur to me now since I was quite fond of a good night's rest but rarely got it. However, there was at least one experience during those years which made such an unusual impression on my sleep-deprived mind that it stands out clearly in memory. Late one night, my bright-eyed baby and I caught the second half of a science fiction rerun on TV which left me with the strangest feeling.

Aboard a spaceship a new game was introduced which rapidly spread among members of the crew. The player wore a headset and played individually, in their mind. The game was highly addictive, stimulating the pleasure centers of the brain, interfering with logic and reasoning abilities, distracting players from their duties—thus leaving the starship vulnerable. It was no surprise to learn at the end that the game had actually been planted by an enemy.

I recall the creepy sensation I had as I watched the crew members fall victim to the debilitating effects of their addiction—to the point where they cared about nothing but playing the game. I wondered if there could ever be a similar real-life situation. See where I'm going with this?

Years later, baby Becca had become a teenager (with a real talent for sleeping). It was a holiday weekend, and all of my kids were begging to see a long-anticipated movie which had just been released. That afternoon, as our family entered the crowded lobby of the complex, we picked up our tickets and headed to the theater where our movie was showing. As we passed hundreds of people waiting

in lines for other shows, I was startled to observe the number of
headphones, earbuds, and electronic devices among the crowd. I'd
estimate that fully 75 percent of the people were talking on cell
phones, texting, playing games, listening to music, e-mailing, or
viewing images on their phones. Most surprising to me was the
number of young children with gaming devices. For such a large
crowd, there was relatively little social interaction. I had a serious chill-
up-my-spine déjà vu moment as my mind flashed back fourteen years
to the TV episode that had troubled me, and I thought, *We're nearly
there.*

Decades ago, in my child development class at BYU, we discussed
toddlers and tantrums. When a child is focused on something you
don't want them to have and they're too young to be reasoned with,
the most effective method of separating them from that object—
while preventing a tantrum—is to distract them and redirect their
attention.

This technique is surprisingly effective with adults too, and Satan
has it down to a science. The adversary now has a boatload of digital
tools at his disposal to assist in the work of distraction: smart phones,
laptops, iPods, iPads, blogging, Facebook, Twitter, Instagram, iTunes,
selfies, web surfing, and video games. These modern tools have
redefined the way we communicate and socialize. The technology is
so impressive, the devices so portable, they can easily lead to trouble.
Elder David A. Bednar has observed, "We live at a time when
technology can be used to replicate reality, to augment reality, and
to create virtual reality."[1] If we aren't actively focusing on living a
virtuous life, we may find that through the unrestrained use of digital
media, we're gradually transitioning into virtual life.

Don't get me wrong—these devices and activities are not
inherently evil. They are sophisticated tools for accessing information;
facilitating communication, studying the gospel, and researching
family history; improving efficiency in our businesses; and providing
appropriate entertainment. But, as Elder Bradley D. Foster said, "A
distraction doesn't have to be evil to be effective."[2] It only needs to
be a distraction. If we're not vigilant, these digital tools can inhibit
or even damage our most important relationships—with our families
and our God.

Wise use of digital tools can be a blessing. It is remarkably easy, however, to allow them to encroach on our relationships before we even recognize what's happening, as illustrated in the following story:

> A man recently walked into a diner with his eyes locked forward while carrying on an animated conversation on his cell phone. A young wife trailed a few steps behind. Soon they were seated. The two perused the menu, placed their orders and, when their food arrived, began eating their lunch. Through it all, the husband never pulled the phone from his ear.
>
> The man's gastronomical multitasking meant a dull lunch for his companion. As he jabbered away between bites, the wife stared straight ahead, keeping silent company with the sandwich and French fries in front of her.
>
> The two didn't swap a single word during the entire meal.
>
> Soon the check arrived, the woman paid the bill, and the couple filed from the diner. The man continued his cell phone call as he steered the family car out of the parking lot and on to the street. Who knows what the call was about? Perhaps the husband was touching base with an old friend. He could have been closing a business deal. Or maybe he was simply yapping with a buddy about last night's ball game.
>
> But consider what was lost. . . . There was likely a time when the couple at the diner counted down the hours between meals together. But that enthusiasm for the other's undivided and deserved attention had cooled—a victim of life's minutia and, on this day, a single cell phone call. One thing is certain: a busy man passed on an opportunity to enjoy a few quiet moments with his mate.[3]

Another danger of digital distractions is the huge chunk of time they can eat out of our day—time that could be put to much better use. When a longtime family friend returned from serving as a mission president, my husband, Brad, took the opportunity to ask President Wilcox to share his number-one piece of advice for teenagers preparing to be effective missionaries. We were startled by his answer. Without hesitation he said, "Lose the video games! Young people entering the mission field will find that impressive hand/eye coordination is not a necessary skill for missionary work." President Wilcox's point was forcefully made. Far too much time is being spent on meaningless or even harmful entertainment, at the expense of developing the spirituality necessary to hasten the work of the Lord. This applies to adults as well.

Women are not immune to digital time-wasters, including gaming. A friend once admitted to me that she was horrified to realize she had become addicted to playing a Super Mario video game and it had become a distraction in her life. Addictions can happen to anyone of any age. Gaming can be as addictive as drugs. We aren't afraid of games, so we don't guard ourselves against them.

As blogging has become a popular activity, many creative folks have begun using their blogs as a sort of family history, complete with pictures. What a fantastic way for extended families to connect with each other. But if we're not careful, checking out others' blogs can encroach on time better spent taking care of our children, improving our relationship with our spouse, magnifying church callings, and studying the gospel. My friend Heather recognized she was engrossed in so many blogs that it was eating up a significant portion of her time. She wisely determined to set aside fifteen minutes daily to catch up on blogs of people closest to her and then move on with her day.

Another aspect of life that has changed with the emergence of digital tools is the easy access they give us to other people. This can be a tremendous blessing when there is an urgent need to contact someone. But this access, if not controlled, can also be an intrusion into our personal lives. It seems that everyone wants instant access to their friends. Between cell phones, e-mail, blogs, and social media websites, we can easily contact others and view whatever information they choose to post. Are we aware that our children also have this access—day or night—to friends or strangers if we allow them unrestricted cell phone and Internet use before they're mature enough to use them responsibly?

While it can be convenient and interesting to keep tabs on each other through texting and social networks, many of us have become so accustomed to instant messaging that we're growing impatient with a God who doesn't always "text back" immediately.

Not only do we have increased access to the lives of friends and family, but the adversary has increased access into *our* lives if we allow it. The day we first connect to the Internet, we open a new portal which allows information to flow both in and out. Many decades ago, if one wanted to get their hands on illicit material, they had to physically go out and search for it. Now, in large measure, *the world has come to us* through the Internet.

Some digital distractions can lead to serious, full-blown addictions. A counselor for LDS Social Services addressed one dangerous trend at a leadership training meeting I attended. In her counseling practice, she noticed a growing problem. When young couples have an argument and are feeling upset with their spouse, it's easy to seek comfort elsewhere by texting or using social media to reconnect to someone with whom they've had a relationship in the past. This always leads to trouble. If you are married, *any* emotionally intimate online or over-the-phone relationship with someone other than your spouse is dangerous. Cyber infidelity can only lead to heartache.

Though many relationships have begun online and resulted in healthy marriages, great caution must be exercised with chat rooms and dating sites since there is an element of anonymity when communicating online, which facilitates deception. Anyone can create a detailed personal profile which may not necessarily be truthful.

Remember the game on the spaceship? Once addicted, the crew members were so focused on playing the game that they failed in their duties on the ship, leaving themselves vulnerable to enemy attack. It's no different for us. Any addiction, no matter how harmless it may appear, increases our vulnerability to the adversary. We cannot afford to relinquish control to him.

Satan is remarkably clever in his attempts to lure careless and unsuspecting people off the strait and narrow path with distractions that are highly addictive, for an addiction is really a form of self-sustaining sin. Once someone is first hooked, they will return again and again on their own—no need to take the trouble of tempting them each time. "And [Satan] had a great chain in his hand, and it veiled the face of the whole earth with darkness; and he looked up and laughed" (Moses 7:26).

One of the greatest dangers of the path into a virtual life is that it frequently leads to pornography. Many people naively believe this is only a man's addiction, but do not be fooled—women are susceptible. We cannot justify the viewing of pornography as natural curiosity or call it by any name that will change the fact that it is damaging and evil and highly addictive. Pornography never strengthened a single family, never improved anyone's quality of life. It must be avoided as the debilitating plague it is.

A major warning flag of addictions is the impulse to cover up our actions. "Every one that doeth evil hateth the light . . . lest his deeds should be reproved" (John 3:20). If we feel the need to hide our actions from family and respected friends, there is a problem. Period. The desire for secrecy occurs when we are living contrary to the light of Christ and is a definite signal that it's time to seek help from the Lord, possibly through the bishop.

I've often wondered why we seem so vulnerable to addictions, and I believe I understand at least one of the reasons. We came from a heavenly place where light—spiritual light—was our natural habitat. Though a veil was drawn over our minds when we entered mortality, we seem to carry with us a deep hunger for light and truth. However, we don't always recognize that hunger for what it is. With our spirits housed in bodies and subject to "the natural man" (Mosiah 3:19), we attempt to fill our *spiritual* hunger by satisfying our *physical* cravings. It is a futile pursuit. "It shall even be as when an hungry man dreameth, and, behold, he eateth; but he awaketh, and his soul is empty: or as when a thirsty man dreameth, and, behold, he drinketh; but he awaketh, and, behold, he is faint, and his soul hath appetite" (Isaiah 29:8). Only the living water of Jesus Christ can quench our thirst.

These days we have easy access to stimulants, whether in the shape of habit-forming drugs and alcohol or the powerfully addicting experiences of a virtual world. While these substances and experiences can momentarily entertain us, provide a brief escape from our troubles, and feed our physical cravings, those who indulge are inevitably left empty and frustrated. In the end we must admit that nothing in the virtual world has the power to satisfy the deep hunger of our spirits.

Hear the strong words of a modern-day Apostle: "Today I raise an apostolic voice of warning about the potentially stifling, suffocating, suppressing, and constraining impact of some kinds of cyberspace interactions and experiences upon our souls. The concerns I raise are not new; they apply equally to other types of media, such as television, movies, and music. But in a cyber-world, these challenges are more pervasive and intense. I plead with you to beware of the sense-dulling and spiritually destructive influence of cyberspace technologies that . . . promote degrading and evil purposes."[4]

Would it surprise us to realize that our addictions to technology and social media are actually our idols? Anything that takes precedence over Christ in our lives is idolatry. Yes, even the harmless-looking smart phone in our hand can fall into that category if misused.

God has commanded that we have no other gods before Him because the moment we place anything above Him in importance, we thwart His work for us. Our ability to draw on Christ's saving power is diminished. And since only He can save us, we are left without help or hope. This is the most serious consequence of turning our hearts to modern-day idols.

A careful study of the Old Testament makes it clear that idol worship became the downfall of entire generations. In biblical times, people were worshiping actual graven images made of wood or stone or precious metals, but our modern-day idols take vastly different forms. They are at least as harmful as their ancient predecessors, even if we don't acknowledge them openly as idols. But "if we have . . . stretched out our hands to a strange god . . . shall not God search this out?" (Psalm 44:20–21).

The Book of Mormon provides a clear way for us to judge our relationship with the digital: "That which is of God inviteth and enticeth to do good continually; wherefore, every thing which inviteth and enticeth to do good, and to love God, and to serve him, is inspired of God" (Moroni 7:13–14).

Sisters, we must refuse to be lured into the traps of a virtual world. The virtual life appeals to many because it seems an easy path.

It seems to require nothing of us, yet it yields heartache, addiction, and deep regret. Elder Bednar offers two questions to help us avoid being caught up in a virtual life:

1. Does the use of various technologies and media invite or impede the constant companionship of the Holy Ghost in your life?

2. Does the time you spend using various technologies and media enlarge or restrict your capacity to live, to love, and to serve in meaningful ways?[5]

Are we willing to analyze our habits relating to our digital devices, asking ourselves if we're allowing our virtual habits to overtake the virtuous ones in our lives? Whether we are simply wasting time or we have slipped into serious addictions, admitting there's a problem will allow us to take the necessary steps to overcome it with the help of the Savior. As we heed the warnings and counsel of our latter-day prophets, we will discover the dignity and peace which come by turning from the virtual to a virtuous life. Then we will be free to bask in "the glorious liberty of the children of God" (Romans 8:21).

Notes

1 David A. Bednar, "Things As They Really Are," CES Fireside, May 2009.

2 Bradley D. Foster, "Mother Told Me," *Ensign*, May 2010.

3 "Things That Matter Most," *Church News* (The Church of Jesus Christ of Latter-day Saints), April 23, 2011.

4 David A. Bednar, "Things As They Really Are," CES Fireside, May 2009.

5 Ibid.

CHAPTER #9
Experience with Light

IT'S SAFE TO SAY THAT the prophet Moses had some extraordinary experiences in his lifetime. In order to preserve his life, he was hidden away for months as a baby. When it was no longer feasible to hide him, he was sent on a little journey down the Nile River in a basket, was raised in the household of an Egyptian pharaoh, had a life-changing encounter with a burning bush, led more than a million Hebrew slaves out of bondage and out of Egypt, and then received the Ten Commandments. Oh yeah, there was also that little incident we call the parting of the Red Sea. These adventures made for some compelling journal entries.

There was another experience, also journal worthy, that we don't refer to as often, but I find it the most powerful of all. This account is found in the first chapter of Moses. "Moses was caught up into an exceedingly high mountain, and he saw God face to face" (Moses 1:1–2). In order for Moses to endure the intensity of God's presence, some of God's glory had to be upon him. Moses was told and shown incredible things worthy of much discussion—but I'll leave that for another day. Let's skip to the part where "the presence of God withdrew from Moses. . . . And as he was left unto himself, he fell unto the earth" (Moses 1:9). We then read this significant statement: "It was for the space of many hours before Moses did again receive his natural strength" (Moses 1:10). Did you catch that? It took *hours* to recover from the presence of such a glorious, light-filled Being.

Not wanting to be outdone, Satan puts in an appearance, tempting Moses to worship him. I love the way Moses responds, basically saying, "Where's your glory? I couldn't even look at God without some of His glory being upon me, but I can look on you with my natural eyes" (see Moses 1:13–14). Moses then declares: "[God's] spirit hath not altogether withdrawn from me . . . and *I can judge between thee and God*" (Moses 1:15, emphasis added). Oh, mark those words with a red pencil. Because of Moses's recent experience with God's light, the Spirit was with him, making it easy for him to see the contrast when faced with darkness.

Few humans will ever experience the two extremes of face-to-face encounters with God and the adversary, but the principle is the same in our less dramatic dealings with good and evil: the more frequent our experiences with light and truth, the greater our ability to discern clever counterfeits. It becomes easier to recognize that, as alluring as evil may appear, it is still just that—evil.

As spirit daughters of God, we are beings of light. We came from a light-filled environment. Perhaps that explains the almost instinctive fear of darkness evident in most small children. "Ye are the children of light, and the children of the day: we are not of the night, nor of darkness" (1 Thessalonians 5:5). Yet, as we are born into mortality, some of that light seems to be "muffled by the coarser elements of the physical body."[1]

Elder Robert D. Hales writes, "As children, we learned how to keep darkness away by turning on a light. Sometimes, when our parents went away for the evening, we would turn on every light in the house! We understood the physical law that is also a spiritual law: Light and darkness cannot occupy the same space at the same time."[2]

A portion of God's light (the light of Christ) has been planted within us, and whenever we are exposed to light and truth, our inner light responds. This is a precious blessing and a protection, but in order to keep that response strong, we must have frequent experiences with light. Then we, like Moses, will clearly see the difference when faced with lesser things.

When was your last experience with light? This morning? Last week? Last year? It's possible to take in just enough spiritual light at church each week to keep us alive, but we'll never truly thrive until we take responsibility for our light levels, actively seeking out experiences that fill us with light and truth. You don't have to look far. If you have a copy of the scriptures, you have access to light; if you know how to pray, you have access to light; if you can fast or serve or go to the temple, you have access to light.

The ceiling fan in our master bedroom has five lightbulbs. One day, as I flipped on the light switch, I saw that the room looked a bit dimmer than usual. Sure enough, when I looked up I could see that one bulb had burned out. Now, I could have changed it right then, but that would have involved walking out to the hall closet where replacement bulbs are kept—like, three whole steps. Then, of course, I'd have to climb up on the bed to reach the fixture. Who has time for all that? With two reading lamps and four recessed lights in the room, I figured I could see well enough. Changing the bulb could wait.

A week later I noticed that the room was significantly dimmer and discovered that another bulb had burned out. This was getting irritating. Not, however, irritating enough to compel me to make the trip down the hall for new bulbs. I lived with this new dimness for several days. Finally, knowing that we had guests coming over and it was possible someone might wander into our bedroom, I mustered the energy to search out some new bulbs and make the change. As it turns out, it wasn't all that hard, and the difference was—forgive me for stating the obvious—like night and day.

In this dispensation of restored truth, we are blessed to have nearly unlimited access to light. Lamps and lightbulbs are not the *source* of physical light—they're powered by electricity. In the same way, the scriptures and the temple are not the light itself but are channels through which light and truth are transmitted—their power originating with the Divine Source of light. We're told, "If your eye be single to my glory, your whole bodies shall be filled with light, and there shall be no darkness in you" (D&C 88:67). As we become bearers of light, other people can literally access light through us when we share our testimonies or teach truth.

So how is your light level today? Are your bulbs fully lit, or are you, like my ceiling fan, two bulbs short of bright? If our light level is gradually decreasing, at what point do we say, "Hey! It's too dim in here!" In order for us to have a regular time to check our light levels, the Lord has kindly given us a commandment to keep the Sabbath day holy.

Wait a second—how does a discussion about light lead into the Sabbath day? Think for a moment. A day of rest from our weekly labors, a day of worshipping the Lord by attending church and studying the gospel—what better time to assess our spiritual health, which is directly linked to our light intake?

My cat, Felix, has mesmerizing golden eyes. I'm fascinated by the change in his pupils according to the play of light in a room. When he turns his head toward a sunny window, his pupils almost disappear, forming mere vertical slits on the golden irises. The reverse is also true. Turning from brightness toward a much dimmer area causes an immediate dilation of the pupils until Felix's eyes appear mostly black with just a thin, gold rim about the outer edge.

Our spirits have the same ability to adapt to changing light levels. Because of the Light of Christ in each of us, when we first turn from light to darkness, it is obvious to us, like entering a dim building after hours spent in full sunlight. This should trigger a flashing red DANGER sign and is a warning for us to turn back to a lighted area. Unfortunately, if we continue in darkness, our spirits will adjust to the lower level of light. As Elder Hales describes it, "We may become accustomed to the dimness of our surroundings and forget how glorious it is to walk in the light."[3]

The opposite effect is felt when turning from darkness to light. Just as our eyes hurt when we step from a darkened movie theater out into a sunny afternoon, spirits that have been "hanging out" in the shadows will experience some discomfort when exposed to brightness. Perhaps it's the sting of guilt. But a willingness to come out from the darkness and seek the light will eventually turn to a craving for its presence. It is worth noting that we will eventually live in a kingdom where we are comfortable with the light level. (See D&C 76:70–78.)

Just as plants use light as an energy source to perform the process of photosynthesis, God's children require frequent exposure to light for spiritual growth. Some things can grow without light—you know, stuff like mildew, mushrooms, and mold—but that's hardly a ringing endorsement for darkness. Who wants to be filled with the equivalent of spiritual fungus?

I love the mental image created by the following example from Elder Hales:

> When I was a boy, I used to ride my bicycle home
> from basketball practice at night. I would connect a

small pear-shaped generator to my bicycle tire. Then as I pedaled, the tire would turn a tiny rotor, which produced electricity and emitted a single, welcome beam of light. It was a simple but effective mechanism. But I had to pedal to make it work! I learned quickly that if I stopped pedaling my bicycle, the light would go out. I also learned that when I was "anxiously engaged" in pedaling, the light would become brighter and the darkness in front of me would be dispelled.

The generation of spiritual light comes from daily spiritual pedaling. It comes from praying, studying the scriptures, fasting, and serving—from living the gospel and obeying the commandments. . . . Sometimes people ask, "Why do I have to go to sacrament meeting?" or "Why do I have to live the Word of Wisdom [or] pay tithing? Why can't I have one foot in Babylon?" May I tell you why? Because spiritual pedaling takes both feet! Unless you are fully engaged in living the gospel—living it with all of your "heart, might, mind and strength"—you cannot generate enough spiritual light to push back the darkness.[4]

How about another lightbulb story? Not only do I love to *see* the temple, I love to clean it. Early one June day, I arrived at the Mount Timpanogos temple to fulfill a cleaning assignment. The small army of men and women assembled there was divided up and dispatched to various areas of the building. I was pleased to be in the group directed to the celestial room.

Our task that morning was to clean the elegant and unique chandelier, which had already been dismantled. Eight tiers' worth of slim glass rods and tiny crystals lay on the sheet-draped furniture around the spacious room. Each volunteer was handed a pair of white cotton gloves and shown the proper way to polish the rods of glass. With hundreds of pieces to clean, this was a time-consuming job— yet there was an element of fascination in it. To handle pieces of the glittering chandelier I had admired for so long felt like a privilege. Once the rods were gleaming, the cleaning brigade moved to the next stage. Rubbing individual crystals between our gloved fingers, we removed every trace of dust. After replacing countless lightbulbs from the interior of the fixture, it was time to reassemble the chandelier. I felt a surge of excitement to be a part of putting it back together and was so engrossed in the process that it wasn't until I stepped away that it occurred to me that the lights weren't on. Though it was still interesting to see it unlit, there was no comparison to the lighted version. I felt like I was looking at a glass sculpture, pretty, but nothing to write home about.

During the two weeks that followed, I waited impatiently while the temple maintenance schedule was completed, feeling unusually eager to be back in the celestial room to see the chandelier fully lit. I was not disappointed! The brilliance of the beautiful fixture, lit from within, was stunning—such a dramatic contrast to the "glass sculpture" version I had seen. The glass rods shone with a golden light, and tiny flashes of color sparkled across the crystals. I could discern every hue of the rainbow.

That's what God's light does for us. It breathes life and color into our ordinary mortal selves. It wakes up our divine nature and beautifies us in a way no earthly substance ever could. And our earthly experience with His light is just a taste of what will follow for those who crave that light and relentlessly pursue it.

Just how bright is God's light? John the Revelator recorded this description of the holy city, or the celestial kingdom: "And the city had no need of the sun . . . to shine in it: for the glory of God did lighten it, and the Lamb is the light thereof" (Revelation 21:23).

Wow. The city had no need of the sun. The glory of God the Father and His Son, Jesus Christ, is that powerful. Sisters, if there is that much light and power and glory available to us, why do we ever dabble in darkness—no matter how attractively it may be packaged? As women who are meant to be bearers of God's light, we must ask ourselves: Am I burning brightly as an example of the believers, or am I flickering?

There is no limit to the amount of light our Heavenly Father will send into our lives once we remove the barriers that hinder its flow, but that is up to us. His light "fill[s] the immensity of space" (D&C 88:12). It is available to anyone who desires to have it. When Jesus declared, "I am the light of the world" (John 8:12), His meaning was much more literal than we probably realize. Because He lived a perfect life, there were no barriers, and thus the light of His Father was able to fill Him perfectly. He literally is the light. "He that receiveth light, and continueth in God, receiveth more light; and that light groweth brighter and brighter until the perfect day" (D&C 50:24).

As we ponder the beauty and power of God's glory and listen to the whisperings of the Holy Spirit, we will become aware of the habits, thoughts, and actions that are preventing us from experiencing a fullness of that marvelous light. Then we can begin breaking down those barriers, until we can say wholeheartedly, "Truly the light is sweet" (Ecclesiastes 11:7).

Notes

1 Brent L. Top and Wendy C. Top, *Glimpses Beyond Death's Door*, (Orem, Utah: Granite, 2005), 54.

2 Robert D. Hales, "Out of Darkness into His Marvelous Light," *Ensign*, May 2002.

3 Ibid.

4 Ibid.

Section Four

FOCUSING OUR EFFORTS

CHAPTER #10
Better Things to Do

I'M REMEMBERING A SUMMER FROM my childhood. Each morning after completing our chores, my brothers and I played out in the sunshine, enjoying our vacation from school. My mother spent her hours tackling housework and laundry, fulfilling her church assignments, typing dissertations for university students, and feeding her hungry children along with any neighbor child who wandered through our kitchen. But at noon each weekday, Mom escaped to the basement—where it was nice and cool—and munched on her sandwich while watching *General Hospital* and *One Life to Live*. (I should add that this was more than four decades ago, when the soaps were both shorter and tamer than today.)

I often joined Mom in front of our little black-and-white TV set. At first I paid little attention to the shows she was watching; I just enjoyed sitting with my mother. Soon, however, I became engrossed in a kidnapping plot which stretched out over many days on *One Life to Live*, eventually becoming so anxious that I began to lose sleep over it.

Fortunately, it didn't take long for Mom to realize what was happening, and though she had enjoyed her shows for several years, she made a decision which turned out to be one of the greatest gifts I ever received from her. She told me we weren't going to watch those programs anymore. She quit her soap opera habit cold turkey that day—knowing that she had better things to do.

I remembered the lesson I learned from my mother's example when, as a full-time missionary, I took the opportunity to show my investigators the film *Man's Search for Happiness*, wherein Elder Richard L. Evans shared this wisdom: "Life offers you two precious gifts—one is time, the other freedom of choice, the freedom to buy with your time what you will. . . . Yours is the freedom to choose. . . . Every day, every hour, every minute of your span of mortal years must sometime be accounted for. And it is in this life that you walk by faith and prove yourself able to choose good over evil, right over wrong, enduring happiness over mere amusement. And your eternal reward will be according to your choosing."[1]

Though my mother and I walked away from soap operas, that didn't mean we gave up TV altogether. On weekday afternoons I could usually be found watching *Gilligan's Island* and *The Brady Bunch* with my brothers before we dug into our homework. On Saturday evenings Mom and I enjoyed *The Lawrence Welk Show* (yes, really), and the whole family enjoyed *Jacques Cousteau* specials and *Mutual of Omaha's Wild Kingdom*. But there came a day when our family experienced what my parents now call a lucky break. The television set broke and we couldn't afford to have it repaired. What a poor, deprived family we were, "suffering" mild withdrawals as we lived without our favorite shows.

Several months later, our parents announced that they had saved enough money to fix the TV. Then they posed a life-changing question: "Do we really want to fix it?"

In the end we chose not to. During the months our TV sat silent in the corner, we found better things to do. We found more time for sports and outdoor activities. We practiced our musical instruments and took family drives in the canyon. Our grades improved as we made homework a priority; family home evenings lasted longer since no one was rushing to catch the last half of *Monday Night Football*. And because we actually talked to each other more, we became acquainted on a deeper level.

We went eight years without a television in our home. Occasionally we saw programs at the houses of friends, and we watched the important stuff like general conference and BYU bowl games at our grandparents' homes. By the time my parents bought another TV set, I was twenty years old. When I was in my thirties, a friend said to me, "I wonder what I was doing as a teenager during all the hours you were practicing the piano." Then she answered herself, "I guess I was probably just watching TV."

I am *not* encouraging everyone to toss their television—obviously there are worthwhile shows to view—but TV was one of the biggest time-wasters of my generation. These days there are more ways to entertain ourselves than we ever dreamed of all those decades ago, giving us more choices as to how we use our time. So how do we choose wisely?

Elder Dallin H. Oaks offers excellent counsel:

> A childhood experience introduced me to the idea that some choices are good but others are better. I lived for two years on a farm. We rarely went to town. Our Christmas shopping was done in the Sears, Roebuck catalog. I spent hours poring over its pages. For the rural families of that day, catalog pages were like the shopping mall or the Internet of our time.
>
> Something about some displays of merchandise in the catalog fixed itself in my mind. There were three degrees of quality: good, better, and best. For example, some men's shoes were labeled good ($1.84), some better ($2.98), and some best ($3.45).
>
> As we consider various choices, we should remember that it is not enough that something is good. Other choices are better, and still others are best. Even though a particular choice is more costly, its far greater value may make it the best choice of all.[2]

Much of what we do with our time will be dictated by the seasons of our lives. For instance, a mother raising young children will, of necessity, spend countless hours feeding, bathing, changing diapers for, doing laundry for, cleaning up after, entertaining, and teaching her children. There will be countless trips to the doctor and dentist, the grocery store and school. Without a doubt there will be long hours in the night, rocking babies and caring for sick children, comforting little ones who had a nightmare, and changing the sheets of a bed wetter. Many of these tasks seem menial, unfulfilling, and even downright unpleasant—but if it is our "season" to raise children, these activities can qualify for the best uses of our time.

We need to be certain that all of our activities—whether related to work or leisure—are *at least* classified in the "good" category. We have better things to do than spend our allotted mortal hours in pursuit of anything that drives the Holy Spirit away. With hundreds of options competing for our time and attention, it is imperative that we analyze the way we use our waking hours, viewing our activities within the framework of good, better, and best. Mentally reviewing our baptismal and temple covenants is an excellent way to see time-wasters for what they really are.

I'd like to share an example of someone who decided to make better use of his time, and the results that flowed from his decision. During his teenage years, John Bytheway had an idea for a book he felt would be helpful to other teenagers. He remembers thinking, at age sixteen, *One day I'll write that book.* Here he tells his own story:

> There I am at BYU and working at Continuing Education, and I thought, *When am I ever gonna do that book?* And then . . . I looked at my day. . . . The only time I could even think of was early in the morning. So I decided I would go to bed at 10:00, and that meant I would miss all that worthwhile channel surfing from ten to midnight that I usually did—the news, Leno, Letterman, whatever was on. What a sacrifice!

For the next month John got out of bed at five, went to his office, and wrote from six to eight each morning. After completing his first chapter, he submitted it to a publisher, who wrote back requesting the rest of the manuscript. For three more months, John persisted in his new writing habit until the manuscript was complete.

> It was a wonderful time in my life. People would say "What are you doing these days?" I didn't define [my life] by the eight hours that I worked, I defined it by those two hours where I had shut off television, traded my least productive time—ten to midnight—for my most productive time—six to eight [in the morning].
>
> I remember one day walking [into a bookstore] and seeing [my book] on the shelf and just thinking, "I wrote that!" Here's my question: let's say I had watched TV for those four months? What would I have to show for it? I can't think of a thing. . . . And then I thought,

Gee, John, here's an idea: why don't you just do this for the rest of your life?"[3]

Don't you love that story? Think of the payoff John received by exchanging his channel surfing for something of far greater worth. Do we claim to be too busy for meaningful prayer and scripture study, yet spend chunks of our day surfing the net, repeatedly checking Facebook, gaming, or watching our favorite programs? It's time to be honest with ourselves about the way we're using our time. Just like spending money, when we spend our time, we should expect to get a valuable return.

Through the years I have tried to teach my children a simple principle about spending money: all purchases are not equal. For instance, we can spend ten dollars on fast food that will be consumed within minutes, or we can spend the same amount to buy a T-shirt that can be worn multiple times—perhaps even for years. We could deposit that ten-dollar bill in a savings account where we can save up for an item we really need. Or we could even donate the money to the Church's Perpetual Education Fund, where it will help improve the quality of life of a deserving person.

This same principle also applies to the different ways we spend our time. If we have an hour "to spare," we might spend it surfing the Internet or watching a low-brow sitcom. Or we could work on our long-desired college degree online or spend that hour prayerfully preparing a lesson for our Primary or Young Women's class. We also have the option of calling a friend who is struggling and could use a sympathetic listener, or reading (or even writing) an inspirational book.

Thousands of hours of our lives are spent doing necessary chores and tasks, such as rotating the laundry, commuting to and from work, or mowing the lawn. We can go about our business with our minds set in neutral, or we can use that time for pondering important questions and gospel principles, or listening to audio recordings of the scriptures and general conference.

Early in my college days, I made the decision to serve a full-time mission. I determined to make the most of my preparation time by taking extra religion classes at BYU. During one semester I signed up for mission prep, teachings of the living prophets, and Book of

Mormon, along with my other general education courses. As a result, I was immersed in the scriptures for a large percentage of my study time. To this day, I consider the study hours of that semester to be one of the greatest investments of time I ever made. Each hour I studied the gospel, I wasn't just spending time, I was investing in my future.

Later, the hours I spent as a missionary in personal and companion gospel study proved to be another significant investment of my time which has paid off repeatedly. In my years of early motherhood, when it seemed next to impossible to sit down with my scriptures in hand, I was grateful that my mind had been filled with the words of the scriptures during previous years of study, and even if I rarely had uninterrupted study time, at least I could ponder gospel principles as I cared for my little ones.

Serving a full-time mission also gave me a taste of what it means to live a consecrated life. What a blessing to have had that experience, for throughout my adult life, when I have found myself caught up in lesser activities, I know there are better things I could be doing.

While we are expected to make good use of our mortal probation, Heavenly Father doesn't require every moment to be spent in hard labor. Elder D. Todd Christofferson speaks of the relationship between work and leisure:

> God has designed this mortal existence to require nearly constant exertion. . . . A consecrated life is filled with work, sometimes repetitive, sometimes menial, sometimes unappreciated, but always work that improves, orders, sustains, lifts, ministers, aspires.
>
> Having spoken in praise of labor, I must also add a kind word for leisure. Just as honest toil gives rest its sweetness, wholesome recreation is the friend and steadying companion of work. Music, literature, art, dance, drama, athletics—all can provide entertainment to enrich one's life and further consecrate it.[4]

The principle of opposition in all things applies to work and leisure. Spending our time in productive ways—working hard for a good cause and rejecting the temptation to constantly be entertained—makes it possible to enjoy whatever leisure time we do have because we've earned the right to take a break from our honest labors. We are able to find joy in simple things. Those who do little meaningful work, on the other hand, overindulging their urge to be entertained, will reach a point at which it is impossible to satisfy their appetite for pleasure. Many of us have yet to learn the lesson that the fruits of honest labor can be vastly more satisfying than any form of entertainment.

If we ever wonder how the Lord feels about the way we spend our days, we might consider the words of Amulek: "For behold, this life is the time for men to prepare to meet God; yea, behold the day of this life is the day for men to perform their labors" (Alma 34:32).

In the words of Ezra Taft Benson: "When we put God first, all other things fall into their proper place or drop out of our lives. Our love of the Lord will govern the claims for our affection, the demands on our time, the interests we pursue, and the order of our priorities."[5]

As we pursue a deeper understanding of the plan of salvation and the true purpose of our life on earth, we will begin to view each hour as the precious gift it is, "the time to prepare to meet God" (Alma 34:32). Then, as we're daily faced with the temptation to spend our time in trivial pursuits, we'll be able to turn away from them, firm in the knowledge that we have better things to do.

Notes

1 *Man's Search for Happiness* (pamphlet, 1969), 4–5.
2 Dallin H. Oaks, "Good, Better, Best," *Ensign*, November 2007.
3 John Bytheway, "Turn off the TV and Get a Life," audio recording.
4 D. Todd Christofferson, "Reflections on a Consecrated Life," *Ensign*, November 2010.
5 Ezra Taft Benson, "The Great Commandment—Love the Lord," *Ensign*, May 1988.

CHAPTER #11
Keeping Sheep

THIS IS THE CHAPTER THAT almost wasn't. The topic is a tender one, which increases the odds of hurting feelings or stepping on toes, and I have no desire to do either. But I find that I can't *not* write about motherhood. The mother in each of us is at the very core of our womanly identity.

The word *mother* is not only a noun but also a verb, meaning "to watch over, nourish, and protect." Many women come to motherhood in less traditional ways than bearing and raising children. Those who teach children in schools and at church, those who take a lonely teenager under their wing, those who model modesty and excellence and who watch over their neighbors—they are mothers indeed.

Sister Sheri L. Dew has stated, "For reasons known to the Lord, some women are required to wait to have children. This delay is not easy for any righteous woman. But the Lord's timetable for each of us does not negate our nature. Some of us, then, must simply find other ways to mother. And all around us are those who need to be loved and led."[1]

Though motherhood can bring deep joy and enrich our lives, I will focus here on some of its challenges. A significant portion of the trials we experience in this life center around our families and motherhood. For example, we might not be blessed with the privilege of marrying, or we're blessed to be married but can't conceive children. We might carry a baby to full term only to have a still birth, or our child may be disabled or die young. Or we bear a healthy child but he has a rebellious spirit as he grows older. We may have many healthy children, but the stress of motherhood takes a heavy toll. The list of possibilities is nearly endless. It is apparent that the home is the laboratory of our lives, and in regard to our families, what doesn't overpower us teaches and even sanctifies us.

If we're not careful, we may injure the tender feelings of other women when we make insensitive remarks or pass judgment on their family situation. Wise sisters remember that *every* woman has her personal trials when it comes to motherhood—even if it is not apparent to outsiders—and surely we have better things to do than add to a sister's heartache by passing judgment on an issue that is none of our business.

For every stay-at-home mom who wishes she "had a life," there is a mother who must work full-time outside the home but would give anything to spend more time with her children.

For every woman in the middle of a miserable, complicated pregnancy, there is a woman who wishes she could carry a baby full term or even conceive a child.

For every woman who mourns the loss of her pre-pregnancy figure, there's a woman who would trade her slim waistline in an instant for the privilege to feel life fluttering within her expanding belly.

For every woman who judges a sister who has been married several years and hasn't yet started a family, there is a sister who sobs into her pillow at night because her pregnancy test came up negative. Again.

For every woman who stands up at the end of the Mother's Day meeting to receive a flower, there is a woman who dreads going to church that day because, for her, it's the most painful Sunday of the year.

For every sleep-deprived mother who has just about had it with the chaos and noise level of her pack of young children, there is a mother who grieves because her disabled child will never be able to run or speak.

On September 23, 1995, I was in the Salt Lake Tabernacle when President Gordon B. Hinckley made the following statement: "We of the First Presidency and the Council of the Twelve Apostles now issue a proclamation to the Church and to the world as a declaration and reaffirmation of standards, doctrines, and practices relative to the family."[2] The prophet then proceeded to read "The Family: A

Proclamation to the World." In the spirit of full disclosure, I must admit I did not initially recognize the value of this document. I recall thinking, *Hmmm . . . of course that's all true, but there's nothing in there we haven't heard before.* My finite little mind completely missed the point.

Who knew that within a relatively short period of time, the values of the world in regard to the family would shift so dramatically? Who, indeed: the prophets, seers, and revelators of our day. If ever we need evidence of the authenticity of their callings, we need look no further than this proclamation and the timing of its publication. As discussed in a previous chapter, widespread use of the Internet has changed the way we exchange and access information, information which influences our values. Much of that information is not in harmony with God's plan for our happiness, presenting a distorted view of motherhood.

The world would tell me that by having a large family I am overpopulating the earth. But according to the proclamation, "God's commandment for His children to multiply and replenish the earth remains in force."[3] The gospel teaches that there are many spirits waiting to be born into mortality and it is a blessing for them to come to a stable, Christ-centered family, where they will be raised as responsible citizens who contribute positively to the world around them. I need not apologize for welcoming them into my home.

The world would tell me that pregnancy will change my figure. No kidding. But must I be ashamed of the stretch marks that formed as my body made room to carry my beautiful babies? Would I really trade my children for a firmer tummy?

The world would tell me that choosing to stay home with my children instead of joining the work force is a waste of a college education. Really? Then can someone explain why I constantly draw upon knowledge I gained in my English, dance, mission prep, Spanish, psychology, child development, music, culture, and religion classes to help my children with homework, have intelligent conversations with them, and encourage them to expand their horizons and develop their talents?

The world would tell me that caring for my children all day leaves little room for personal growth or expression. Even within the Church, there are some who take exception to the idea that "mothers are primarily responsible for the nurture of their children," as if raising children were a demeaning, brainless alternative to a fulfilling life.[4] As I embarked on my adventure as a mother, I was completely unprepared for the education I was about to receive. My tiny teachers have given me countless opportunities to develop patience, tolerance, empathy, and unconditional love. As I've taught basic gospel principles to my children, my own understanding has deepened significantly. I've become a whiz at multitasking, and I've learned a few lessons about exhibiting grace under pressure (though I'm still perfecting my technique). My strengths and weaknesses have been revealed to me with startling clarity. Most importantly, the struggles and heartaches of raising teenagers have provided me with life-changing lessons about the power and breadth of the Atonement of Jesus Christ.

The world would tell me that by choosing to stay home with my children, I am limiting my ability to influence the world in a significant way. I disagree. I recently welcomed my oldest daughter and son back from full-time missions to the Philippines and Brazil, and sent another son off to Mexico City for two years.

Speaking of righteous mothers, Sister Julie B. Beck has said, "Their goal is to prepare a rising generation of children who will take the gospel of Jesus Christ into the entire world. Their goal is to prepare future fathers and mothers who will be builders of the Lord's kingdom for the next fifty years. That is influence; that is power."[5] I'm just beginning to understand the scope of influence that I, through my work as a mother, can have in the community and even in the world.

Elder M. Russell Ballard has stated, "Today our society is bombarded with messages about womanhood and motherhood that are dangerously and wickedly wrong."[6] One of the most dangerous of these messages is that choosing to be a mother and staying home to raise children is somehow a lesser life experience than using our skills out in the work force.

For those mothers who work outside the home because there is no other option, you have no cause to add guilt to your already heavy burdens. You know who you are, and so does your Heavenly Father. As stated in the proclamation: "Disability, death, or other circumstances may necessitate individual adaptation."[7] Years ago, I admired a single mother in my ward who was raising and providing for seven children, working long hours as a nurse. Her children, five of whom were teenagers, were quite impressive. I asked this good lady her secret for raising such a great bunch of kids while dealing with the stress of a full-time job and shouldering the staggering responsibilities of parenthood alone. She said, "The Lord is aware of us. He knows I would stay home with my children if I could, but since I must earn a living, He compensates. He has worked miracles for us. He has raised up good people in the ward and fine teachers at school to be mentors and examples for my family."

Sister Julie B. Beck shared this insight,

> One of the questions that I get frequently is, "Is it okay if I work outside of my home?" You have to know that as an international, global, Relief Society president, that question isn't always appropriate in all of the world's countries. There are many, many places where if our women don't work, they don't eat. So of course they have to work. The question of whether or not to work is the wrong question. The question is, "Am I aligned with the Lord's vision of me and what He needs me to become and the roles and responsibilities He gave me in heaven that are not negotiable? Am I aligned with that, or am I trying to escape my duties?"[8]

If mothers are working outside the home to provide "extras" and not just the necessities of life, it would be wise to consider the counsel of the prophets and other leaders who have encouraged mothers to stay at home wherever possible.

> Fathers and mothers, before you decide you need a second income and that mother must go to work out of the home, may I plead with you: first go to the Lord in prayer and receive his divine approbation. Be sure he says yes. Mothers with children and teenagers at home, before you go out of your homes to work, please count the cost as carefully as you count the profit.[9]

My own mother faced this dilemma. Here is her story, in her own words:

I had always planned to be home with my children, but when, after six years of marriage, we moved to Indiana so my husband could attend graduate school, I couldn't see how we could get by without my working at least part time. With a heavy heart I applied for work at a pharmacy which was located right next to the old army barracks buildings where the married students lived, and I was hired. During the few days before I was to start my job, I prayed earnestly to know if I was doing the right thing. As I looked at our three little children and tried to imagine some other mother in our compound caring for them while I worked, a strong impression came to me that there had to be some other way—the price of leaving them was too high. I called the pharmacy and told them I would not be able to work for them after all.

Once that decision was made, I could see clearly what I needed to do. I put a notice on the laundry bulletin board and soon had three of our neighbors' little children to tend each day while they went to work! Soon I had six-year-old twin boys to tend for two hours after school. It was a lively group when added to our own children, but babysitting provided us with the income to pay for our fifty-dollar-per-month apartment. Best of all, I was at home with my own children.

Since I had some free time in the evenings, I decided to also do typing in my home for university professors and students. After the children were in bed, I would begin typing theses, dissertations, and term papers while Doug was at the library studying. Decades later, some of our children said the sound of the typewriter was like a lullaby assuring them that I was there. I knew the decision to stay home had been the correct one for me.[10]

Motherhood is not for the faint of heart. My years as a young mother of five were, by far, the most physically taxing of my life.

Pregnancy and nursing and sleep deprivation can take a significant toll on even the healthiest body. I can totally relate to this observation of Sister Julie B. Beck: "I learned something from my father-in-law years ago. He was a steel-worker and spent his life working three different shifts. He either worked the day shift, the afternoon shift, or the night shift. As a young mother I realized one time that I was working all three shifts, and that's why I was so tired."[11]

In the early years of motherhood, as I sat in sacrament meeting each week, I occasionally looked up toward the stand where my husband was seated with the bishopric. Though I never said it out loud, I confess I often wondered if the bishop could possibly need Brad more than our wiggly, noisy gaggle of children did. I escaped with my young crew to the "cry room" at church more than once not because my *babies* were crying but because *I* was.

There's nothing glamorous about being late for the kindergarten carpool of child #1 because you're changing the toxic diaper of child #3 while vomiting into a waste basket because you're experiencing severe nausea with pregnancy #4, all the while *strongly* suspecting that child number #2 is playing in the toilet. For those who have been granted the privilege of raising children, our challenge is to embrace the experience with its unique (and sometimes even icky) challenges by viewing motherhood with an eternal perspective.

When we're basically running on fumes during the physically demanding years of motherhood, it may seem there is no time for meaningful prayer and scripture study—yet we desperately need the strength they provide. As a young, sleep-deprived mother, I struggled to keep up with my gospel study. In the rare moments I had to sit down alone, I would eagerly open my scriptures, only to nod off after reading just a verse or two. I often knelt to pray with similar results. But I believed that the Lord, who commanded His children to pray and search the scriptures, would somehow prepare a way for me to accomplish it (see 1 Nephi 3:7).

After pondering this matter, I made a helpful discovery: the Book of Mormon on tape. (Yes, tape. I am a dinosaur.) I kept a tape recorder in my bathroom so I could listen to the scriptures while getting ready in the morning. Of course, there were repeated interruptions with babies and toddlers, but as I persisted, I seemed to reconnect with the

Lord. I also learned that Heavenly Father hears the prayers a mother breathes over her nursing baby or tantrum-throwing two-year-old just as surely as He hears the prayers she says when kneeling.

Motherhood can seem unrewarding if we're used to measuring progress on a daily basis or expecting kudos for a job well done. Our little ones don't generally compliment us on the way we fixed the macaroni and cheese or notice our impressive skills when we're juggling car seats, diaper bags, groceries, and uncooperative offspring simultaneously. Perhaps the most frustrating realization of motherhood is that you can't close up shop each night, putting thoughts of work out of mind until it's time to clock in the next morning. Truly, a mother's work is never done.

It's also difficult to feel we have skills and talents that seem to be set aside for a season. My mother wrote to me about a sister in this situation: "My friend has a very talented daughter who has performed for the last ten years in community theater. Now she has a little daughter and has set her performing aside, but she really misses it."[12]

I remember how frustrating it is to feel like you have no outlet for your talents—at least not in the way you've used them before. The year between my mission and my wedding, I discovered a love of songwriting, but when the babies came in quick succession and my husband was frequently away from home fulfilling church assignments, there was little time to explore that interest. What I know now that I didn't understand in the middle of the diaper years was that every time I put my children first I was learning patience and unselfishness. By following the prophet's counsel to stay home with my children, I was practicing obedience, and every time I magnified whichever church calling was mine I was developing my talents. My wise father calls those years the "research phase" for everything I am doing now. In preparing lessons for Young Women and Relief Society, I was writing bits and pieces which would someday appear in the book I didn't know I would write. As the stake music chairman, I discovered that I enjoyed arranging music and the tight sheet-music budget could be stretched if I arranged hymns myself. When there was finally a time for me to compose music, I had something much deeper to say than in my earlier songs, and it seemed I could not write fast enough as the ideas flowed.

For example, one day I was in a songwriting mood—itching to write but with no ideas for a topic. After restlessly pacing around the house for half an hour, I flopped down on the edge of my bed, empty notebook in hand, and stared out the bay window at our pasture. The scruffy winter wool of our small flock of sheep stood out against the dark-red shed. Weary of my fruitless search for a topic, I shifted my focus to the animals. It had been a while since I'd taken a long look at them, and I was surprised to realize they were full grown. When had that happened?

Two springs earlier, a friend had mentioned that his father raised sheep, and each year there were "bummer lambs," whose mothers had died or had twin or triplet births and couldn't feed all their newborns. Jeremy told us we were welcome to come choose some lambs to take home and raise, and we thought it would be a great opportunity for our children. What a sweet experience awaited us as we drove that frigid morning to a high mountain valley to meet our new wooly babies. There are few sights as charming as day-old lambs, bleating and leaping on their spindly little legs. We let the kids pick four of them to bring home.

Four times a day, armed with bottles, we trudged out to the old turkey pen that served as a shelter for our hungry lambs. They sucked so greedily that they occasionally pulled the bottles right out of our hands; all the while their long tails wiggled in rhythm with their eager mouths. Looking out my window twenty months later, I realized how much I missed those days. I felt a surprisingly strong urge to bottle-feed lambs again, to stroke their woolly little heads and marvel again at the coarse texture. How strange that some of those sheep now looked to be the size of the love seat in our family room.

My mind didn't dwell on the sheep for long. Suddenly I was seeing the pasture through a blur of tears as I thought of my little human flock, which was growing at least as fast as the animals. My heart ached as I pictured each of my children and how changed they were from their baby days. Of course I've loved them at every age, but I couldn't help imagining how sweet it would be to hold them again—tiny, toothless, and so soft in my arms. The intensity of my longing was startling. (I suppose that's why the Lord "invented" grandchildren.) It occurred to me that the perfect song topic was staring me in the face. I opened my notebook and began scribbling:

Keeping Sheep

I have a little flock of sheep
and they are mine to tend and keep,
and I must guard them every day
for little lambs, when left alone, will lose their way.

So many voices say to me,
"A sheep fold is no place to be.
your time in there is dull and slow,
and lambs leave very little room for you to grow."

Oh, if I ever start to stray,
deceived by thoughts of greener pastures,
remind me, Lord, that keeping sheep
will lead to happier ever afters.

Oh, surely there will come a day
when all the lambs have left my side
and I am free to roam about
and go exploring other meadows, green and wide.

Yet, something whispers in my heart
that when my sheep have left this pen
I'll long to stroke their little heads,
to draw them close to me and have them young again.

So, if I ever start to stray,
deceived by thoughts of greener pastures,
remind me, Lord, that keeping sheep
will lead to happier ever afters.[13]

For years it seemed I was drowning in diapers, but somehow when I wasn't looking we slipped into a new stage, one where I could leave the house without an industrial-sized diaper bag. The stage where I rarely had to help anyone get dressed, and more often than not, everyone slept through the night. YES! While much about this new stage was exciting for me, it was sobering to realize that since my oldest child was nearing her teens, my influence on her might begin to decrease as she was exposed to more and more new ideas and standards, some of which might not coincide with the teachings she had received at home. I felt as if the winds of change were suddenly blowing around my family, leaving me with a sense of urgency to focus on my children for the short time they would be in my care.

I have benefitted tremendously from the example of my own mother, who embraced the scriptural wisdom "to every thing there is a season, and a time to every purpose under the heaven" (Ecclesiastes 3:1). As the mother of five children, she devoted herself to our care, taking up the burden of earning part of our family's living—as mentioned previously—while my father was juggling his graduate studies and part-time jobs. My mother suffered the disappointment of miscarriages, grieved the loss of her youngest baby, and opened her home and heart to numerous foster children through the years.

As her children grew older and more independent, Mom was able to develop her many musical talents more fully by accepting various church assignments. As she magnified her callings, opportunities she had never dreamed of opened up to her. Always, however, she kept motherhood as her top priority—knowing that her teenagers needed her at least as much as her little ones had. Finally, as her children began to leave the nest, she was free to pursue her interests in new and exciting ways.

During the autumn of her life, Mom has been blessed beyond her expectations, partly because she did everything according to its proper season. As she wrote in one of her songs, "Each season has its own rewards."[14] Without even intending to, Mom found herself in charge of her own music company, and no one was more surprised than she when her local chamber of commerce honored her as Businesswoman of the Year. Later, she and my father served a full-time mission in Chile. Afterward they spent four years as Church service missionaries in a Hispanic ward in their community. Her hard-won ability to speak a new language opened up another season for her, filled with sweet new friendships. I'm still startled to hear her break into Spanish when her friends call or visit.

After discovering a lack of pianists in the local Spanish wards, Mom offered to teach free piano lessons to Hispanic children if they would commit to practice seriously. Through her efforts, several of these children—now teenagers—serve as ward pianists. My mother has discovered the truthfulness of the words, "He hath made every thing beautiful in his time" (Ecclesiastes 3:11).

Lately, I find myself thinking of the story of the prophet Nehemiah. President Dieter F. Uchtdorf shares this account:

> Nehemiah of the Old Testament is a great example of staying focused and committed to an important task. Nehemiah was an Israelite who lived in exile in Babylon. . . . One day the king . . . gave Nehemiah the authority to return to Jerusalem and rebuild the city. However, not everyone was happy with this plan. In fact, several rulers who lived near Jerusalem . . . "took great indignation, and mocked the Jews."
>
> Fearless, Nehemiah did not allow the opposition to distract him. Instead, he organized his resources and manpower and moved forward rebuilding the city. . . . But as the walls of the city began to rise, opposition intensified. Nehemiah's enemies threatened, conspired, and ridiculed. Their threats were very real. . . . As the work continued, Nehemiah's enemies . . . entreated him to leave the safety of the city and meet with them under the pretense of resolving the conflict, but Nehemiah knew that their intent was to do him harm. Each time they approached him, he responded with the same answer: "I am doing a great work, so that I cannot come down" (Nehemiah 6:3).
>
> What a remarkable response! With that clear and unchanging purpose of heart and mind, with that great resolve, the walls of Jerusalem rose until they were rebuilt in an astonishing fifty-two days. Nehemiah refused to allow distractions to prevent him from doing what the Lord wanted him to do.[15]

Let us embrace and honor the different seasons of motherhood. In the midst of our mothering, if we are ever "deceived by thoughts of greener pastures," let us have the strength to say, like the prophet Nehemiah, "I am doing a great work. . . . I cannot come down"

(Nehemiah 6:3). Let us refuse to allow distractions to prevent us from fulfilling our God-given responsibility to mother.

> "So while they still are in my care,
> I pray that I will clearly see
> these little lambs within my fold
> are tender gifts the Master Shepherd has given me."[16]

Notes

1 Sheri L. Dew, "Are We Not All Mothers?" *Ensign*, November 2001.
2 Gordon B. Hinckley, "Stand Strong against the Wiles of the World," *Ensign*, November 1995.
3 Ibid.
4 Ibid.
5 Julie B. Beck, "Mothers Who Know," *Ensign*, November 2007.
6 M. Russell Ballard, "Mothers and Daughters," *Ensign*, May 2010.
7 Gordon B. Hinckley, "Stand Strong against the Wiles of the World," *Ensign*, November 1995.
8 Julie B. Beck, BYU Women's Conference 2011, lds.org.
9 H. Burke Petersen, "Mother, Catch the Vision of Your Call," *Ensign*, May 1974, emphasis added.
10 Janice Kapp Perry, personal correspondence.
11 Julie B. Beck, BYU Women's Conference 2010, lds.org.
12 Janice Kapp Perry, personal correspondence.
13 Lynne Perry Christofferson, "Keeping Sheep," *Keeping Sheep*, (album), 2001.
14 Janice Kapp Perry, "The Seasons of My Life," *When I Feel His Love*, (album), 2005.
15 Dieter F. Uchtdorf, "We Are Doing a Great Work and Cannot Come Down," *Ensign*, May 2009.
16 Lynne Perry Christofferson, "Keeping Sheep," *Keeping Sheep*, (album), 2001.

CHAPTER #12
Serious about Perfection

On a Saturday evening in autumn, I drove to a nearby city to attend a broadcast of the general Relief Society meeting with my mother. The spirit of the messages and music left me with a softened heart and a desire to do better. While I was driving home afterward, my mind begin processing what I had heard and felt. As is usually the case with me, my desire to be a more righteous woman led to thoughts of perfection, inevitably leading to discouragement for a mere mortal gal such as myself.

As my car whizzed along the freeway, my eye briefly caught on the words of a billboard: "Serious about perfection." I didn't quite catch what the sign was advertising, but the phrase lodged itself in my mind, and I pondered it repeatedly over the next few days, asking myself, "Am I serious about perfection?"

If I added up all of the hours from my past which were consumed by fear, guilt, and worry over my lack of perfection, I have no doubt the sum would equal years—years of my life wasted due to a faulty understanding of the Atonement, including the misconception that Heavenly Father demanded perfection of me immediately. On countless occasions I stressed over the fact that my life could end at any time and I would die without having repented of every speck of sin and certainly without having attained a perfect state. I thought that this constant anxiety over my sins and weaknesses was evidence that I was serious about perfection.

In recent years, candid discussions with numerous friends and relatives have revealed that I had been part of a club with many miserable members: The Perfectionists. The only membership requirement was to continually flog ourselves with thoughts of our unworthiness before the Lord who commanded us all to be perfect (see Matthew 5:48). Was my club membership proof that I was serious about perfection? Or does being serious about perfection involve a completely different mindset?

The scriptures reveal that "[Satan] seeketh that all men might be miserable like unto himself" (2 Nephi 2:27). Ironically, one of his most effective methods of ensuring our misery is to promote perfectionism—a distortion of the Savior's plan of repentance and change through His atoning power and grace.

While reading *The Autobiography of Benjamin Franklin*, I came across a quote which was oddly comforting to me. It showed that even Benjamin Franklin, as impressive a person as he was, also struggled with the process of perfection. He wrote,

> I conceiv'd the bold and arduous project of arriving at moral perfection. I wish'd to live without committing any fault at any time. . . . As I knew, or thought I knew, what was right and wrong, I did not see why I might not always do the one and avoid the other. But I soon found I had undertaken a task of more difficulty than I had imagined. While my care was employ'd in guarding against one fault, I was often surprised by another; habit took the advantage of inattention. . . . I concluded, at length, that the mere speculative conviction that it was our interest to be completely virtuous, was not sufficient to prevent our slipping.[1]

Anyone who has undertaken the daunting task of striving for perfection can relate to Mr. Franklin's statement, "I was surprised to find myself fuller of faults than I had imagined."[2]

Why is the prospect of perfecting ourselves so daunting? Perhaps it's because it's not our job. What? But the Savior said, "Be ye therefore perfect" (Matthew 5:48). Yes, but He never said we must accomplish that task by ourselves. He stated His job plainly: "For behold, this is my work and my glory—to bring to pass the immortality and eternal life of man" (Moses 1:39). That's His job. Not ours.

So what is our job? Our job is to come to Christ and be *willing* to be perfected by Him. The day we recognize that the Lord is not asking us to achieve a perfect state through sheer willpower, we can lay aside a tremendous amount of guilt. And the day we move out of the way so the Savior has room to do His job, we take huge steps toward our ultimate goal. When we are serious about perfection, we understand the difference between our role and His in the process.

In the closing verses of the Book of Mormon, the prophet Moroni wrote, "Yea, come unto Christ, and be perfected in him, and deny yourselves of all ungodliness . . . then is his grace sufficient for you" (Moroni 10:32). There's the formula. We come to Christ, work earnestly at repenting and denying ourselves of evil influences, and He perfects us.

When we are serious about perfection, we determine what in our life is ungodly—what creates a barrier between us and the Holy Spirit—and then make it our daily quest to pull the barriers down. When we are serious about perfection, we relieve ourselves of the self-imposed responsibility of judging others. This leaves us with much more time to "work out [our] own salvation with fear and trembling before [God]" (Mormon 9:27). Our belief that Christ can perfect us grows in direct proportion to our understanding of who He is and what the Atonement means.

In our quest for perfection, it is essential that we gain a clear understanding of what sin and weakness really are. In her book, *Weakness Is Not Sin*, author Wendy Ulrich makes an important distinction between the two. "We mistakenly lump sin and weakness together and assume that guilt and shame are the appropriate response to both. . . . Sin and weakness are very different. They have different origins and different consequences, call for different remedies, evoke different responses from heaven, reside in different aspects of our being, and produce different effects. Sin can take us to hell. Weakness can take us to heaven."[3]

Such a bold statement—and a careful study of the scriptures confirms its truth. The Lord declared, "I give unto men weakness that they may be humble" (Ether 12:27).

Sister Ulrich further states, "In other words, weakness is not just a choice we make (as sin is); weakness means vulnerabilities and limitations we must sometimes learn to live with, even as we try to improve, grow, and learn."[4] Because of this the Lord says, "I will be merciful unto your weakness" (D&C 38:14). Indeed, as Elder Richard G. Scott points out, "When the Lord speaks of weaknesses it is always with mercy."[5]

We will always have the nagging feeling that we should do better, be better. This instinctive yearning for perfection is evidence of our divine roots. We are spiritual beings temporarily housed in mortal bodies—a bit like wearing an ill-fitting suit. As magnificent and capable as our bodies are, they are still mortal, subject to illness and fatigue and sharp cravings. The spark of divinity in us will always be at odds with our mortal tendencies, which may explain some of the restlessness and dissatisfaction we feel even when we are diligent in our efforts to repent of our sins and are chipping away at our personal weaknesses.

How thankful I am that perfection is not a requirement for entering the temple; otherwise our recommend interview would consist of only one question, and our beautiful temples would stand empty. But our priesthood leaders do not ask, "Are you perfect?" For now, it is enough to establish our worthiness.

Occasionally, we make the mistake of projecting our mortal weaknesses onto the Savior, assuming that because *we've* not yet learned to love unconditionally, *He* can't possibly love us in all our weakness and impurity. This is a dangerous lie. Because the Savior is already perfect, He loves perfectly. As Paul said, "I am persuaded, that neither death, nor life, nor angels, nor principalities, nor powers, nor things present, nor things to come, nor height, nor depth, nor any other creature, shall be able to separate us from the love of God, which is in Christ Jesus our Lord" (Romans 8:38–39).

Remember the childhood game "he loves me, he loves me not"? The next time you pick a flower, try visualizing Jesus in your mind as you pluck off each petal, declaring, "He loves me. He loves me. He loves me . . ." There is no "He loves me not" with Jesus. He loves me. He loves you. He loves us even if we overeat during the holidays. He loves us when we're cranky with our neighbor or impatient with our child. He loves us though we're lazy or selfish or proud or vain, or if the lesson we taught on Sunday fell flat. He loves us when our latest attempt to overcome a pesky weakness doesn't even last until noon. He loves us even when we don't love Him back. His love does not diminish even when we have committed a serious sin. And because He loves us, He hopes we'll do better tomorrow. But even if we don't, guess what? He will still love us. Remembering the constancy of the Savior's love can keep us from debilitating discouragement in times of weakness.

So why the quest for perfection if the Savior already loves us? Because He wants us to experience the freedom and power that come from overcoming our weaknesses and forsaking sin. He wants us to return to Him and enjoy every blessing He has offered, and in order to do that we must be pure. "No unclean thing can dwell with God" (1 Nephi 10:21).

If we've hesitated in turning to the Lord for help because we're ashamed or fear the process of repenting, perhaps we've misunderstood what repentance is all about. I love the following hopeful statement of Elder D. Todd Christofferson: "Repentance is a divine gift, and there should be a smile on our faces when we speak of it. It points us to freedom, confidence, and peace. Rather than interrupting the celebration, the gift of repentance is the cause for true celebration."[6]

If we're intimidated by the thought of perfection, perhaps we could focus on another *P* word: *progression*. Progression toward perfection. Elder Merrill J. Bateman addressed the frustration we sometimes feel when change and improvement come too slowly for our liking. "Few mortals share with Alma the Younger or Paul the Apostle the dramatic experiences which resulted in their spiritual rebirths over short periods of time. In fact, I believe those experiences are recorded in the scriptures not to define the time frame during which one may be reborn but to provide a vivid picture of what the accumulated, subtle changes are that take place in a faithful person over a lifetime."[7]

The word *progression* puts me in mind of caterpillars and butterflies. Every butterfly begins its life as a tiny egg, and each egg hatches a caterpillar so small it can barely be seen. The newborn caterpillars grow rapidly, constantly feeding on leaves.

Caterpillars face a challenge as they grow: their skin does not stretch with them. So they grow a larger skin under the old one—sort of like wearing a poufy parka crammed beneath a skintight T-shirt.

When the time is right, the old skin is shed, and a new, larger version is exposed. Over the next few weeks, this process is repeated several times.

When a caterpillar molts for the final time, it attaches itself to the stem of a plant. This time, underneath the old skin is a jade-green casing which hardens around the caterpillar and is called a chrysalis. From the outside, it appears that the chrysalis is at rest. However, dramatic changes are occurring inside as the tissues of the caterpillar completely break down and reorganize. The chewing mouthparts are transformed into a straw-like tongue that will be used to sip nectar from flowers. Antennae and wings are developed, until finally, what was once a creeping, chewing insect emerges as a magnificent, fully formed butterfly.

It seems to me that the natural man in each of us is something like a caterpillar, a bit sluggish, doing little but feeding itself, and without even a hint of butterfly evident in its features or actions. Yet every caterpillar has the potential to be a butterfly if it will only endure the molting and chrysalis phases of the life cycle.

The Lord requires us to exert ourselves in the quest for perfection. Every attempt we make to repent, to obey, to improve, brings the caterpillar forcefully to mind. We can almost feel the outer layer of skin sloughing off, making room for the larger version. And sometimes, after we've made significant spiritual progress, it can feel as if we're beginning to grow wings.

Catherine Thomas, former professor of ancient scripture at BYU, calls the Book of Mormon "the manual for the mighty change." She explains, "Over and over again the book reveals the means by which transformations are brought to pass. . . . How many varied and beautiful accounts there are of God touching Man and causing the layers of the old self to fall away?"[8]

The metamorphosis from caterpillar to butterfly takes only a matter of weeks. For us, the process of subduing the natural man will take more than a lifetime. We are less likely to feel impatient when we have a way to measure our progress. Elder Dallin H. Oaks shares two ways we can do this: First, "if we are losing our desire to do evil, we are progressing toward our heavenly goal." Second, "persons who are proceeding toward the needed conversion are beginning to see things as our Heavenly Father sees them. They are hearing His voice instead of the voice of the world, and they are doing things in His ways instead of by the ways of the world."[9]

It is the third week of January as I write this. The mountain valley where I live has experienced nearly two weeks of an unrelenting inversion, which means we're living in a filthy fog, accompanied by bitterly cold temperatures. Adding to the depressing feel of this foggy existence, sunset comes far too early—as it always does in the heart of winter. But just this evening, my daughter Kate pointed out that it's actually staying light a bit longer now. Peering through the window at six p.m., when night has usually set in, I see that Kate is right. Though it's definitely dim outside, it's not yet fully dark.

Each December, we northern-hemisphere-dwellers experience the shortest day of the year, when the sun takes its lowest path across the sky. But the very next day, a quiet phenomenon occurs while most of us aren't paying attention: gradually, in tiny increments, the days begin to lengthen. By the spring equinox, our sunsets will be noticeably later, and toward the end of June it will seem that the sun is content to hang in the sky indefinitely.

As mortals dealing daily with the effects of the Fall, we experience a spiritual inversion—a dim and uncomfortable fog. We grapple hourly with our weaknesses and suffer the shame that comes with sinning. But no matter how far gone we think we are, change will begin as we reach out to the Savior for help and grace. Because our initial attempts to improve are so incremental, we will likely not even notice a change at first. But one day, awareness will begin to dawn: the light is changing, increasing. This is the beautiful process of perfection. Change and improvement come slowly, but they will come. In the dead of winter, summer may seem like a distant dream, but early spring is not so far away, and we can rejoice, even now, in a daily increase of light—however modest. Just as the longest winter nights give way to spring and finally to full summer sunshine, we will someday bask in the fullness of the light within us.

Elder Matthew O. Richardson shared a personal experience that increases my hope of reaching perfection someday.

Many years ago my children and I hiked to the top of South Sister, a 10,358 foot (3,157 m) mountain in Oregon. After several hours we encountered a long forty-five-degree slope of tiny volcanic pebbles. With the summit in sight, we pressed on only to find that with every step, our feet would sink in the pebbles, causing us to slide backward several inches. My twelve-year-old son forged ahead as I stayed with my eight-year-old daughter. Fatigue and discouragement soon set in, and she was heartbroken, thinking that she might not join her brother at the top. My first impulse was to carry her. My spirit was willing, but sadly my flesh was weak. We sat down on the rocks, assessed our situation, and devised a new plan. I told her to put her hands in my back pants pockets, hold on tight, and—most important—as soon as I lifted my foot to take a step, she should quickly put her foot in its place. She mirrored my every move and relied on the lift that came from hanging on to my pockets. After what seemed like an eternity, we made it to the top of the mountain. Her expression of triumph and satisfaction was priceless.

Elder Richardson continues,

I know that your quest to improve may seem overwhelming at times. Please do not become discouraged with your progress. I think back on my experience hiking with my children. We agreed that every time we stopped to catch our breath, rather than focusing exclusively on how much farther we needed to go, we would immediately turn around and look down the mountain. We would take in the scenery and say to each other, "Look how far we've come." Then we would take a deep breath, quickly turn, face uphill, and start climbing again one step at a time.[10]

Allowing ourselves the small victory phrase "look how far we've come" is a healthy way of acknowledging our progress, no matter how small, and strengthening our belief that we can, with the help of Jesus Christ, scale the next slope of our current mountain. We can "continue in patience until [we] are perfected" (D&C 67:13).

Sisters, isn't it time we cancel our membership in The Perfectionists Club? The moment we demonstrate our faith by humbly turning toward the Lord in repentance or seeking divine help in making "weak things become strong" (Ether 12:27), we are changing our spiritual trajectory. In that moment, we become serious about perfection.

Notes

1 Benjamin Franklin, *The Autobiography of Benjamin Franklin*, (Lexington: SoHo Books, 2012), 71.

2 Ibid., 76.

3 Wendy Ulrich, *Weakness Is Not Sin*, (Salt Lake City: Deseret Book, 2009), 3.

4 Ibid, 32.

5 Richard G. Scott, "Personal Strength through the Atonement of Jesus Christ," *Ensign*, October 2013.

6 D. Todd Christofferson, "The Divine Gift of Repentance," *Ensign*, November 2011.

7 Merrill J. Bateman, "Living a Christ-Centered Life," *Ensign*, January 1999.

8 Catherine Thomas, *Light in the Wilderness*, (Provo: Amalphi Publishing, 2008), 222.

9 Dallin H. Oaks, "The Challenge to Become," *Ensign*, November 2000.

10 Matthew O. Richardson, "Teaching after the Manner of the Spirit," *Ensign*, November 2011, emphasis added.

CONCLUSION
Sisters, Arise!

WE STARTED WITH WIMPLES AND crisping pins. We've talked of modesty, makeovers, and motherhood, of technology and temples, and then moved on to thoughts of perfection. Where do we go from here? What kind of women does the Lord need us to be in these latter days? President Boyd K. Packer has declared, "We need women with the gift of discernment who can view the trends in the world and detect those that, however popular, are shallow or dangerous."[1] Our prophets have asked us to step forward, to be distinct and different in happy ways.

Sisters, how will we rise up to fulfill this request? We begin by seeking a true understanding of our divine nature and by embracing our origins. We arise by honoring our bodies and viewing them as instruments of progression. We arise as we shield our spirits from the fiery darts of the adversary, by accessing the protection that comes through obedience and temple worship. We arise when we focus our efforts on pursuits of eternal import as defined by the covenants we've made.

It is clear that attacks against the Lord's standard of morality, the family unit, and the restored Church are increasing. We need not fear, however, because as covenant-keeping women, we have access to tremendous power. We've been called to actively defend our faith, never forgetting that we truly stand for Christ only when we declare our beliefs in a Christlike manner. We are promised that as we dare to stand for truth and righteousness, the Holy Ghost will magnify our influence for good in surprising ways. It is time to stand courageously and unapologetically for the doctrine of Jesus Christ.

Sisters, arise!

Notes

1. Boyd K. Packer, "The Relief Society," *Ensign*, Nov. 1978, 8.

For the music to "Keeping Sheep" and "Sisters, Arise!" please visit christoffersonmusic.com.

AUTHOR BIO

LYNNE PERRY CHRISTOFFERSON WAS RAISED in the Rocky Mountains; served as a missionary in Washington, D.C.; and has worked as a freelance musician. She received her education at Brigham Young University prior to pursuing full-time the "double major" of marriage and motherhood. Somewhere between mission and marriage, she discovered a love of songwriting. Her compositions and arrangements have received awards on local, Church, and national levels, and can be found on her albums *Keeping Sheep* and *Lift Your Mind Higher*, among others. In recent years her love of penning gospel-centered lyrics and her thirst for the written word have morphed into the writing of inspirational prose. She and her husband, Bradley Christofferson, are the parents of five children. Lynne enjoys reading, bottle-feeding lambs, hiking, and exploring Southern Utah's red-rock country.